BRAIN
GAMES
FOR
BRIGHT
SPARKS

Puzzles and solutions by
Dr Gareth Moore
B.Sc (Hons) M.Phil Ph.D

Illustrations by Jess Bradley

Designed by Zoe Bradley

Edited by Sue McMillan and Katy Lennon

Cover design by John Bigwood

BRAIN GAMES
FOR
BRIGHT SPARKS

BUSTER BOOKS

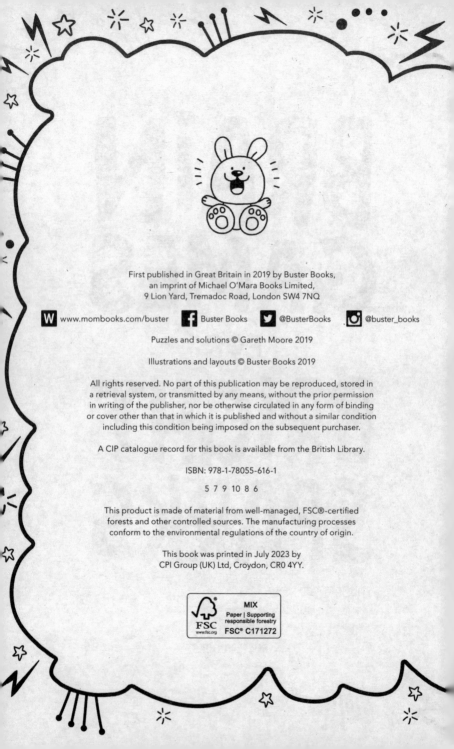

First published in Great Britain in 2019 by Buster Books,
an imprint of Michael O'Mara Books Limited,
9 Lion Yard, Tremadoc Road, London SW4 7NQ

W www.mombooks.com/buster   f Buster Books   ✗ @BusterBooks   ◯ @buster_books

Puzzles and solutions © Gareth Moore 2019

Illustrations and layouts © Buster Books 2019

A CIP catalogue record for this book is available from the British Library.

ISBN: 978-1-78055-616-1

5 7 9 10 8 6

This product is made of material from well-managed, FSC®-certified
forests and other controlled sources. The manufacturing processes
conform to the environmental regulations of the country of origin.

This book was printed in July 2023 by
CPI Group (UK) Ltd, Croydon, CR0 4YY.

MIX
Paper | Supporting
responsible forestry
FSC® C171272

INTRODUCTION

It's time to get your mind ready for this brilliant brain game book, with more than 80 puzzles to test your knowledge and skills.

The puzzles get harder as the book progresses, so it's best to start at the beginning and work your way through. You'll see a little clock symbol at the bottom of each puzzle. Use this space to record how long each brain game takes you to complete.

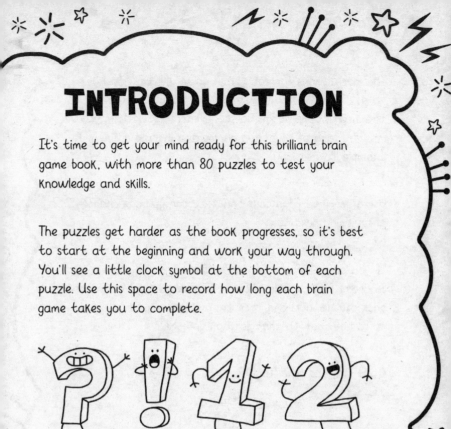

There's plenty of space on the pages to make notes as you go, but if you need more room to work out your answers, use the blank pages at the back of the book.

The instructions for each brain game will tell you how to get started. If you're not sure what to do, read the instructions again, to see if there's something you've missed. Many of the brain games also include a finished example to help you.

The instructions for each brain game will tell you how to get started. If you're not sure what to do, read the instructions again, to see if there's something you've missed. Many of the brain games also include a finished example to help you.

Use a pencil to fill in your answers, then you can change them if you need to.

If you are still stuck, you could also try asking a grown-up. If you're REALLY stuck, have a peek at the answers in the back of the book, and then try and work out how you could have got to that solution yourself.

Good luck and have fun!

Introducing the Brain Games Master:
Gareth Moore, B.Sc (Hons) M.Phil Ph.D

Dr Gareth Moore is an Ace Puzzler and author of many puzzle and brain-training books.

He created online brain-training site, BrainedUp.com, and runs the online puzzle site, PuzzleMix.com. Gareth has a Ph.D from the University of Cambridge, where he taught machines to understand spoken English.

DOTTY DOMINOES

Complete this loop by placing six dominoes into the shaded spaces. The end of each domino must be placed next to another with the same number of spots. You can only use the dominoes at the bottom of the page to fill the gaps.

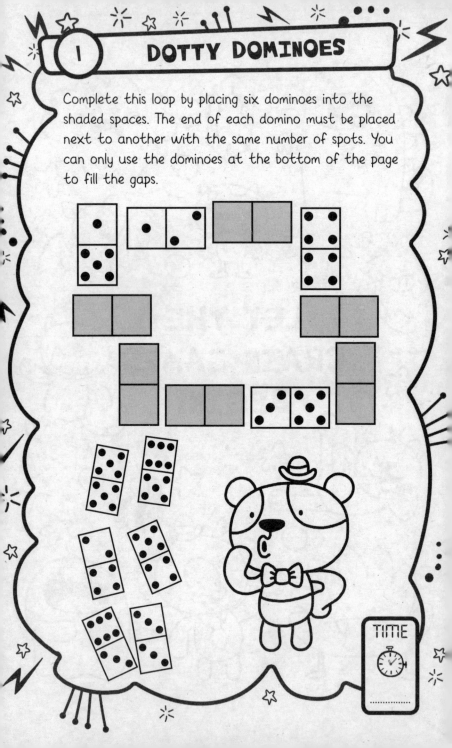

TIME

CRISS-CROSS PUZZLE

Test your word wizardry by filling in this criss-cross puzzle. Cross off each word once it has been used. They can be written horizontally or vertically. One word has been added to get you started.

P I N E A P P L E

three letters
eat
emu
nun
opt
owe
rat

five letters
apple
canoe
error
music
press
scare

nine letters
marmalade
~~pineapple~~
sandpaper
tarantula

TIME

....

TREAT CALCULATOR

3

Can you work out these chocolate calculations?

1. Four friends share ten pieces of chocolate equally, taking as many pieces as they can. The pieces cannot be broken into smaller ones and some may be left over.

HOW MANY PIECES ...

a. ... does each friend have? ....

b. ... are left over? ....

2. Three friends share a chocolate bar. They've each taken four pieces and there are two pieces left over.

What was the total number of pieces in the bar before it was shared?

....

TIME

....

It's time to be a number detective! Can you find the sneaky numbers hidden in each of these words? The letters are in the correct order so you don't have to rearrange them to find the numbers.

EXAMPLE: of<u>ten</u> = ten

1. actioned = ...

2. artwork = ...

3. tennis = ...

4. underweight = ...

5. feminine = ...

6. trustworthy = ...

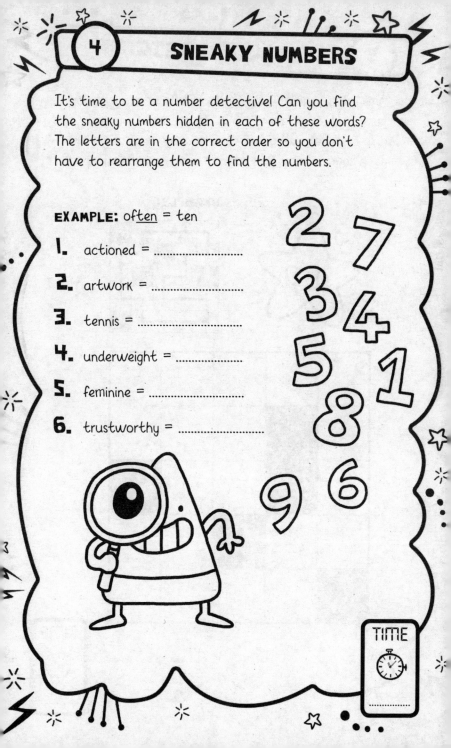

TIME

....

LOOP LOGIC

Are you a star at drawing loops? Draw a single loop passing through every white square. Your moves must only be horizontal or vertical and you can only visit each square once. You cannot cross over the loop.

EXAMPLE:

TIME

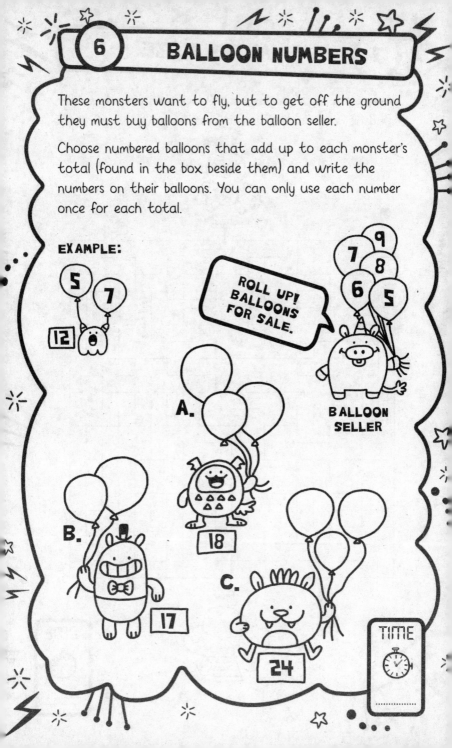

6 BALLOON NUMBERS

These monsters want to fly, but to get off the ground they must buy balloons from the balloon seller.

Choose numbered balloons that add up to each monster's total (found in the box beside them) and write the numbers on their balloons. You can only use each number once for each total.

EXAMPLE:

5   7
12

ROLL UP! BALLOONS FOR SALE.

7 9 8 6 5

BALLOON SELLER

A.
18

B.
17

C.
24

TIME

SPOT THE DIFFERENCE

Can you spot five differences between these two pictures?

BOX THE DOTS

Draw a loop that passes through all the dots. You can only use horizontal or vertical lines and cannot cross over the loop. Some parts have been drawn in for you.

EXAMPLE:

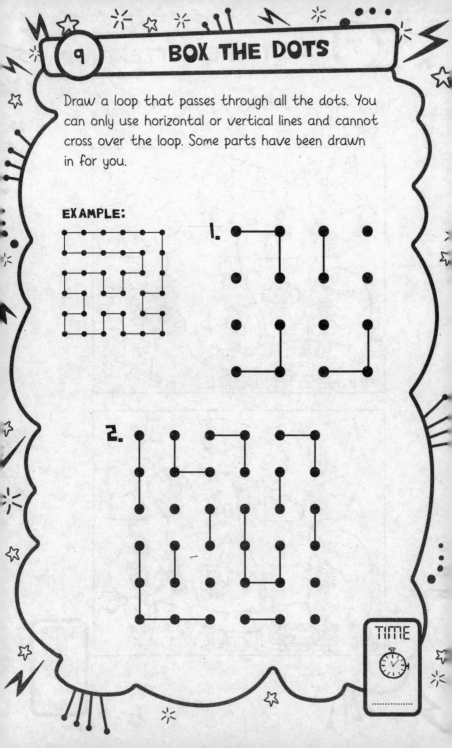

1.

2.

TIME

MIRROR MAGIC

Can you master mirror images? Choose the correct mirror image for shapes 1, 2 and 3 from options a, b and c and circle your answer. You can use a mirror to help you if you get stuck.

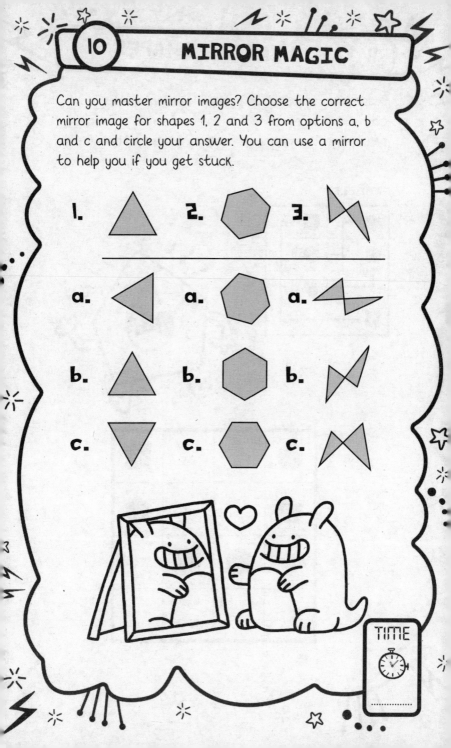

TIME

Draw lines to join each pair of identical shapes. Lines must be horizontal or vertical, with just one per square. Lines cannot cross over each other.

EXAMPLE:

1.

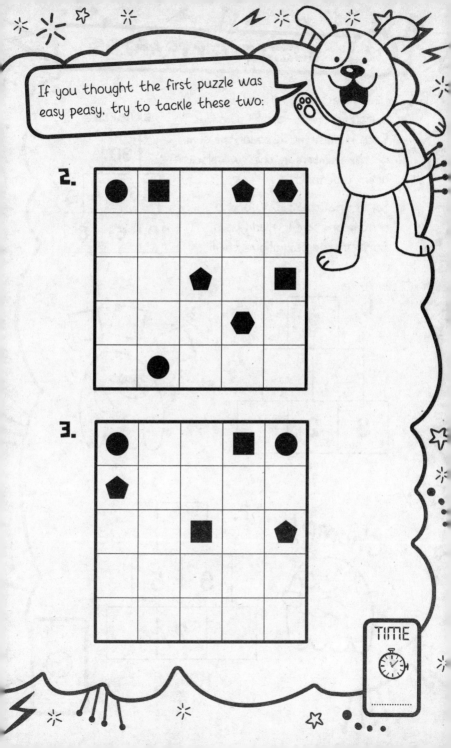

PUZZLING PYRAMIDS

Fill in the empty squares to complete these number pyramids. Each number must equal the sum of the numbers in the two blocks directly beneath.

So, in the example, 10 and 6 on the bottom line add up to 16 in the box above them.

EXAMPLE:

30	
16	14
10	6	8

I.

	9	
3	2	

2.

6	5	
	2	

Chomp!

TIME

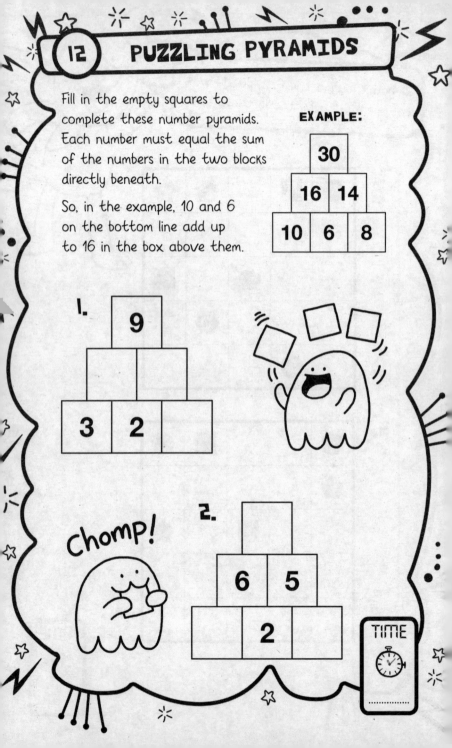

DOGGY DIVISION

13

Draw two straight lines to divide the garden into four areas. Each area should contain a dog, a bone and a water bowl.

TIME

LIVELY LETTERDOKU

Want to be a letterdoku whizz? See if you can fill in the grid so that the letters A, B, C and D appear once in every row and column.

TIME
....

ODD ONE OUT

Can you circle the odd one out in each of the following sets? In the example, 'doughnut' is the odd one out because all of the rest are drinks, while a doughnut is a type of food.

EXAMPLE:

(doughnut)   milk   water   juice

1. mouse   rat   gerbil   lion

2. cluck   quack   bark   cheep

3. bicycle   motorbike   van   tractor

4. sun   lightbulb   hole   flame

Ting-a-ling!

TIME

LETTER MIX

How do you turn a DOG into a GOD? By mixing the letters up, of course! This is an example of an 'anagram'. Write an anagram for each of the words in capitals to complete the sentences.

EXAMPLE:

My play DEN is at one <u>END</u> of the living room.

1. I hit the ball into the NET .... times.

2. The OWL swooped .... under the branches.

3. When he SAW she .... sad, he gave her a hug.

4. I put the lid on TOP of the ....

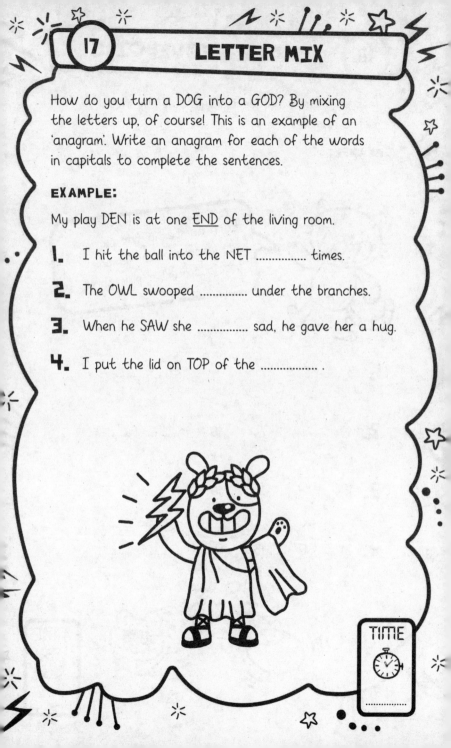

TIME

....

SUPER SEQUENCING

Test your super sequencing skills by filling in the missing numbers.

EXAMPLE:

| 2 | 5 | 8 | 11 | 14 | ...17... |

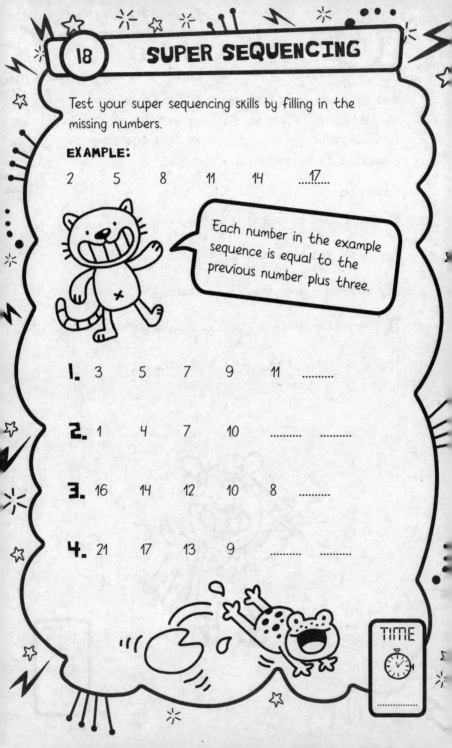

Each number in the example sequence is equal to the previous number plus three.

1. 3   5   7   9   11   ....

2. 1   4   7   10   ....

3. 16   14   12   10   8   ....

4. 21   17   13   9   ....

TIME

....

SPOT THE DOTS

Draw lines between the dots to create a picture. Start at number one then add three to find the next dot. Keep adding three and joining dots until you have completed the image.

•10
1•

•16   •13
4•   •7
•31   •19 •34   22•

•28   25•

TIME

SUPER SUDOKU

This super sudoku challenge will really test your brain power. Place the numbers 1 to 4 into the grids so they appear once in every row, column and marked 2 x 2 area.

A 2 x 2 area has been circled on the example to help you.

EXAMPLE:

4	3	1	2
2	1	3	4
3	2	4	1
1	4	2	3

I.

		4	
1	4	2	
	3	1	4
	1		

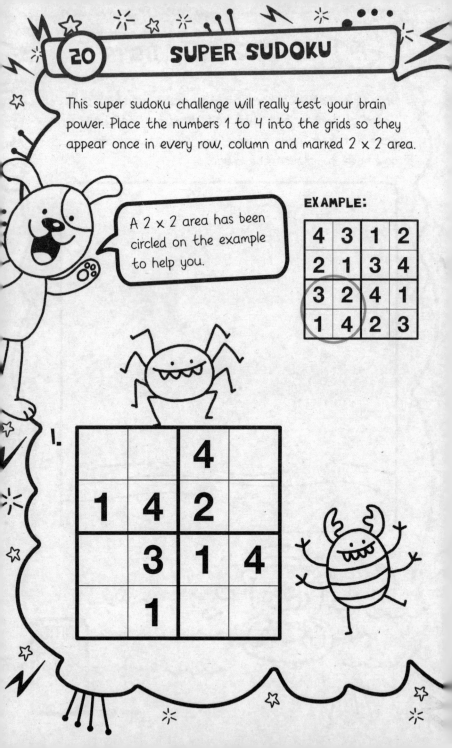

2.

	3	1	
2			3
3			1
	2	3	

3.

	2		
			2
3			
		1	

TIME

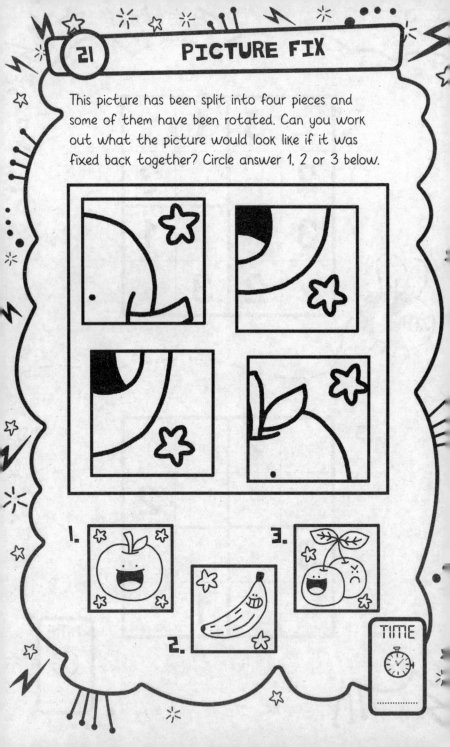

PICTURE FIX

21

This picture has been split into four pieces and some of them have been rotated. Can you work out what the picture would look like if it was fixed back together? Circle answer 1, 2 or 3 below.

1.

2.

3.

TIME

WORD WIZARDRY

Use your amazing word skills to solve this criss-cross puzzle. Cross off each word once it has been used. Words can be written horizontally or vertically. Two letters have been added to get you started.

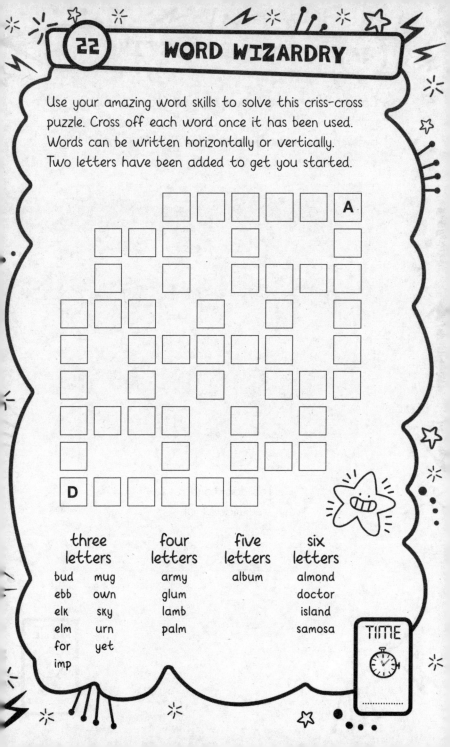

| | | | | | **A** |

| **D** | | | | |

three letters		four letters	five letters	six letters
bud	mug	army	album	almond
ebb	own	glum		doctor
elk	sky	lamb		island
elm	urn	palm		samosa
for	yet			
imp				

TIME

Can you work out what this dot-to-dot puzzle will reveal before you join the dots? Write your answer in the space below, then join the dots to see if you are correct.

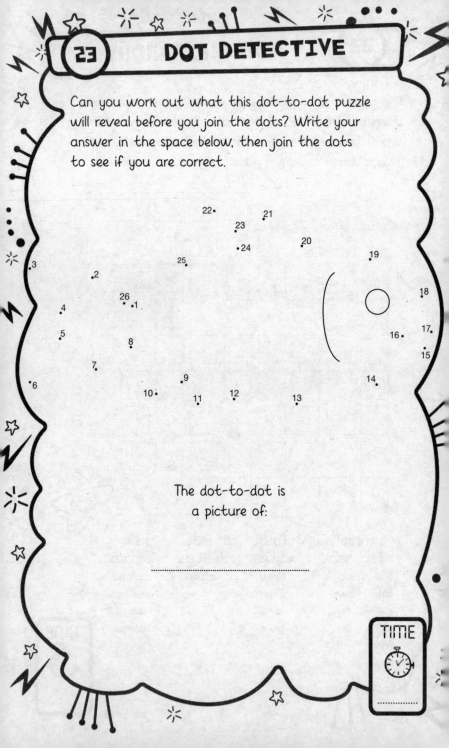

The dot-to-dot is
a picture of:

....

TIME

BODY BASICS

How well do you know your knee from your ankle, or your wrist from your elbow? Draw lines to link each word to the correct location of the body part on the picture below.

ankle

brain

heart

jaw

palm

thigh

TIME

SQUARE SEARCH

How many squares can you spot contained in the shape below? Look closely, the squares differ in size and some may overlap, too.

Write your answer here:

.... squares

TIME

....

SHAPE SPOT

All the following shapes, except one, have something in common. Can you work out which shape is the odd one out? Once you've done so, circle the shape that is different.

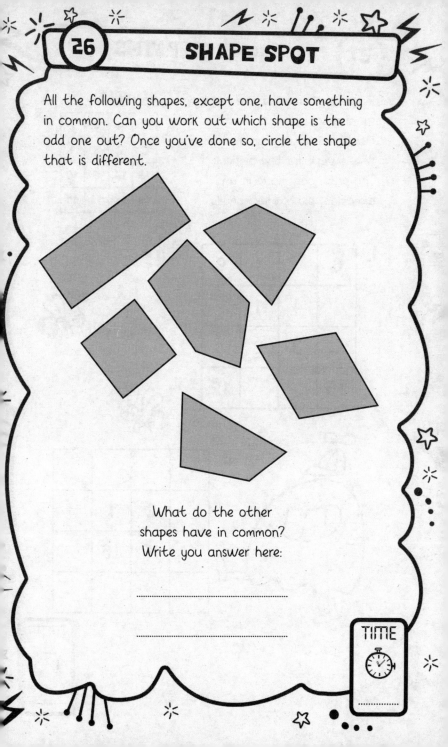

What do the other
shapes have in common?
Write you answer here:

....

....

TIME

Place numbers into the empty squares so the grids contain the numbers 1-16 in a path from the lowest to the highest. The path can move in any direction, except diagonally.

EXAMPLE:

5	4	3	2
6	7	8	1
15	14	9	10
16	13	12	11

1.

6			9
	4	1	
	3	2	
15			12

2.

	2	1	
	15	16	

TIME

SUPER SETS

Place each of the following eight words into one of the two sets, so that each set contains four words. Choose carefully, as one word could go in either set. The first word has been done for you.

bat   ball   ~~boot~~   dog

lion   mouse   net   racket

SET 1: sports equipment   **SET 2:** animals

boot ....

....

....

....

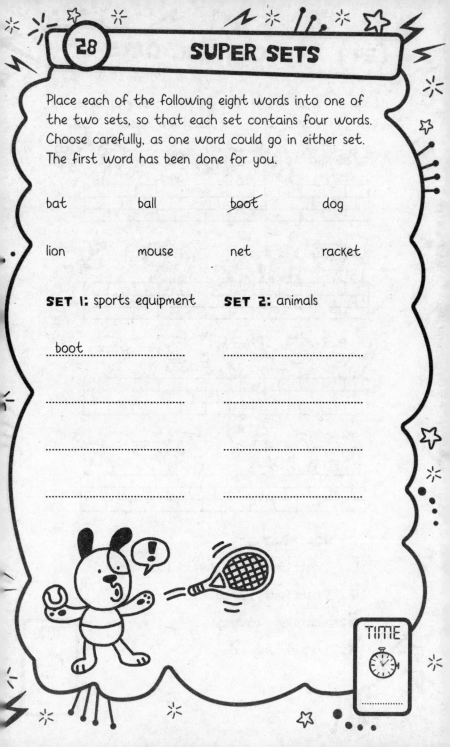

TIME

COUNTING CATS

Look at all of these cats! By paying careful attention, can you answer all of the questions below?

HOW MANY ...

1. ... cats are standing on all four legs? ....

2. ... cats with striped tails are sleeping? ....

3. ... cats are washing? ....

4. ... are chasing mice? ....

TIME

....

You have two different types of chocolate bar. Can you use the following clues to work out how many pieces are in each type of bar?

If you have the following three bars, then you know:

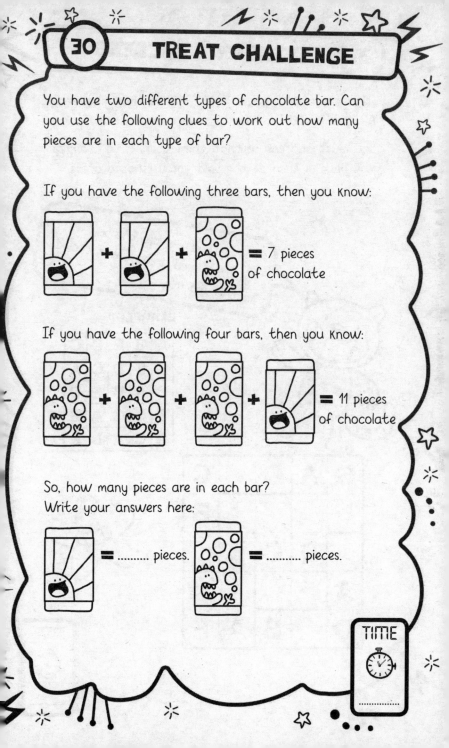

= 7 pieces of chocolate

If you have the following four bars, then you know:

= 11 pieces of chocolate

So, how many pieces are in each bar?
Write your answers here:

= .... pieces.   = ... pieces.

TIME

JIGSAW CHALLENGE

Fill in the empty spaces in the grid so that the letters A, B, C, D and E appear once in every row and column.

You must also ensure that the letters A to E appear just once in each of the bold, jigsaw-shaped areas.

To help you identify the bold jigsaw-shaped areas, one is circled in the example.

EXAMPLE:

A	B	E	D	C
B	E	D	C	A
C	A	B	E	D
E	D	C	A	B
D	C	A	B	E

B	A	D		C
				B
	D	C	B	
A				
D		B	A	E

TIME
....

There are several different words hidden in this word circle. Every word you find in the word circle must use the middle letter, 'A', plus two or more of the other letters.

EXAMPLE:

T + A + N = TAN

Find more words in the circle by solving these clues:

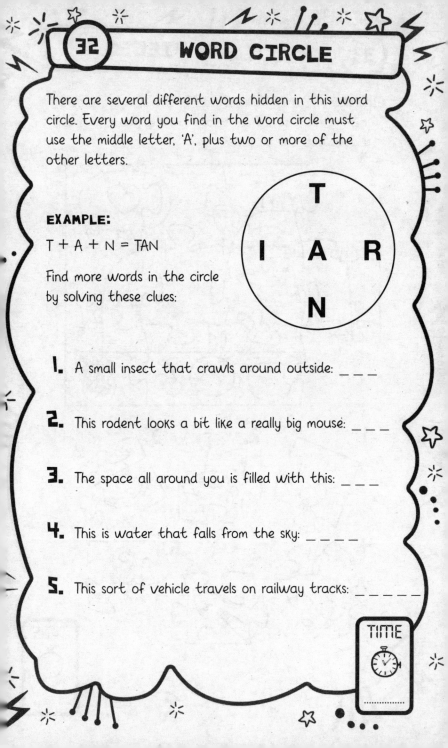

T
I A R
N

1. A small insect that crawls around outside: _ _ _

2. This rodent looks a bit like a really big mouse: _ _ _

3. The space all around you is filled with this: _ _ _

4. This is water that falls from the sky: _ _ _ _

5. This sort of vehicle travels on railway tracks: _ _ _ _ _

TIME

....

JIGSAW PIECES

This jigsaw puzzle is almost done. Can you work out which three pieces from below will fit into the spaces to complete the picture?

1.

2.

3.

4.

5.

6.

TIME

....

TOY BALANCE

You have an action figure, a robot and a toy car. You want to find out which is the lightest and which is the heaviest. This is what you see when you place them on some balance scales:

CAN YOU WORK OUT WHICH IS ...

1. ... the heaviest toy: ....

2. ... the lightest toy: ....

TIME

....

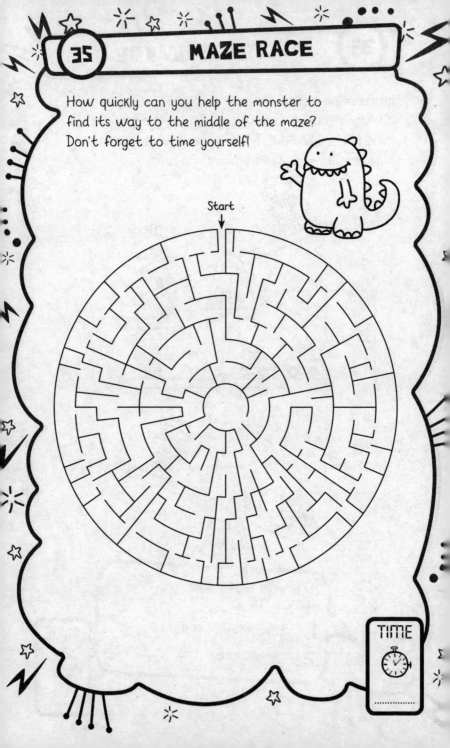

MAZE RACE

35

How quickly can you help the monster to find its way to the middle of the maze? Don't forget to time yourself!

Start

TIME

COIN HUNT

Can you find the gold coins hidden in the empty squares in these puzzles? The numbers in the grid tell you how many coins are hidden in the squares, horizontally, vertically and diagonally next to them. The example shows you how it works.

EXAMPLE:

1	1	2	1
	🪙	2	🪙
2	3		2
🪙	2	🪙	

1.

	2	
2	3	2
		1

2.

	2	2	2
1			
2		4	3
			1

TIME

....

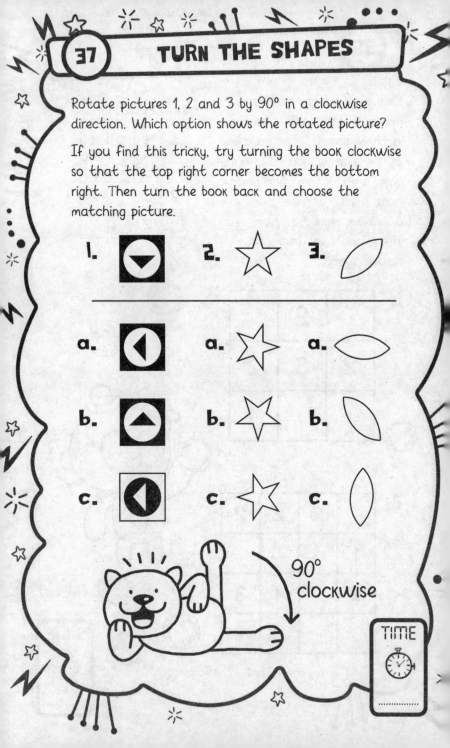

CODE CRACKER

Decode this secret message to find out where an important parcel is hidden. To crack the code, replace each letter in the message with the one immediately before it in the alphabet.

So, for example, replace B with A, and K with J. Use the alphabet at the bottom of the page to help you.

VOEFS UIF
UBMM PBL
USFF

WRITE YOUR ANSWER HERE:

_ _ _ _ _   _ _ _   _ _ _ _   _ _ _   _ _ _ _

A B C D E F G H I
J K L M N O P Q R
S T U V W X Y Z

TIME

FLOWER POWER

These special number flowers need to be arranged in the vases. Pick the correct flowers from the choices below and draw them into each vase so that they add up to the total written on it. Only use each flower once per vase.

3 5 6 10 9

A. 12

B. 16

C. 20

D. 30

TIME

DOMINO LOOP

Complete this loop by placing six dominoes into the shaded spaces. The end of each domino must be placed next to another with the same number of spots. You can only use the dominoes at the bottom of the page to fill the gaps. Which domino doesn't fit in the loop?

TIME

Can you solve the clues to complete this crossword puzzle? To help you, the number in brackets after the clue tells you how many letters the answer has.

Write your answers in the grid starting from the square that matches the clue number. Write 'across' answers horizontally and 'down' answers vertically.

ACROSS

1. Ancient Egyptian King (7)

2. Shake with fear (7)

3. Straighten or extend a part of the body (7)

DOWN

4. Really wanting a drink (7)

5. Loud musical instrument (7)

6. Gather a number of things together (7)

If you're stuck, try another clue. The answer might fill in some letters in the tricky word to help you work it out.

TIME

....

PICTURE MYSTERY

Follow the rules below to shade in some squares in the grid. What simple picture does it reveal?

1	2	3	4	5
6	7	8	9	10
11	12	13	14	15
16	17	18	19	20
21	22	23	24	25

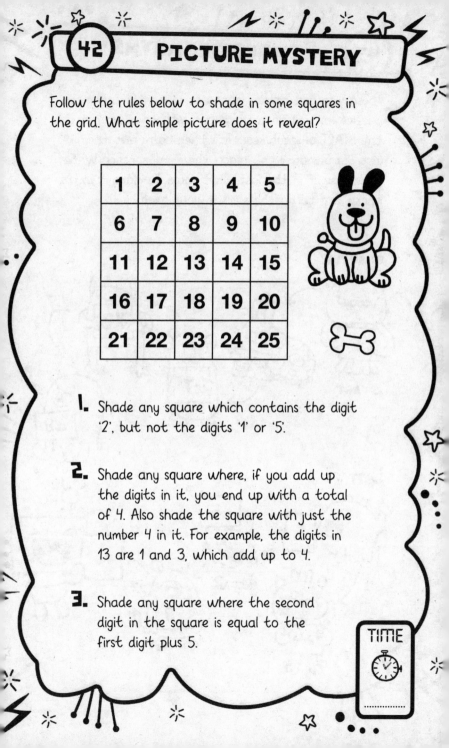

1. Shade any square which contains the digit '2', but not the digits '1' or '5'.

2. Shade any square where, if you add up the digits in it, you end up with a total of 4. Also shade the square with just the number 4 in it. For example, the digits in 13 are 1 and 3, which add up to 4.

3. Shade any square where the second digit in the square is equal to the first digit plus 5.

TIME

MONSTER MATHS

These monsters have created some mental arithmetic puzzles for you to solve. Begin with the number at the START of each sequence then carry out the instructions until you reach the final monster. Write your answer in the last empty box. To make it extra tricky, try to do the sums in your head.

EXAMPLE:

5 START +6 -7 X2 =8

1. START

6 +4 +5 -8 =

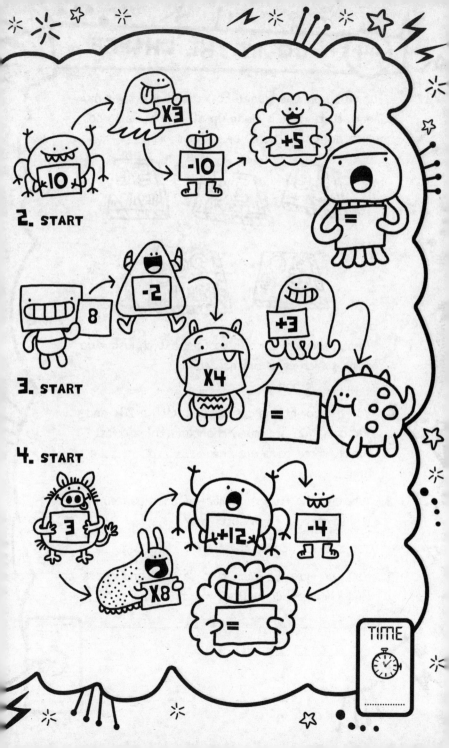

2. START

3. START

4. START

TIME

Far away on the planet Eos, they have their own money system. It is made up of the following coins, which are called 'Eons', or 'e' for short.

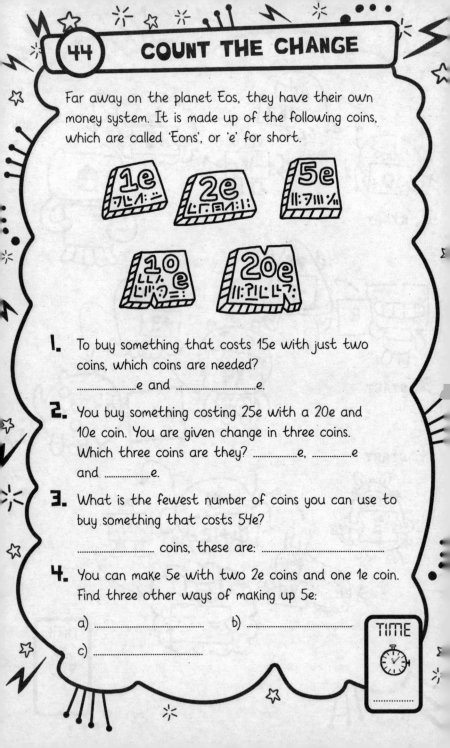

1. To buy something that costs 15e with just two coins, which coins are needed?

........................e and ....e.

2. You buy something costing 25e with a 20e and 10e coin. You are given change in three coins. Which three coins are they? ....e, ...e and ....e.

3. What is the fewest number of coins you can use to buy something that costs 54e?

.... coins, these are: ....

4. You can make 5e with two 2e coins and one 1e coin. Find three other ways of making up 5e:

a) ....   b) ....

c) ....

TIME

....

MIRROR IMAGES

Imagine the horizontal line under these three shapes is a mirror. Work out which of the options, a, b or c, would be the result of reflecting each shape? You can use a mirror to help you if you get stuck.

1. **2.** **3.**

a. **a.** **a.**

b. **b.** **b.**

c. **c.** **c.**

TIME

ODD-EVEN SUDOKU

Can you solve these two unusual sudoku puzzles? Place numbers from 1 to 4 in the empty squares for the first puzzle (and numbers from 1 to 6 for the second) so that each row, column and bold-lined box contains one of each number. Even numbers (2, 4 or 6) must be placed in a shaded square. The example shows you how it's done.

EXAMPLE:

1	3	4	2
4	2	1	3
2	1	3	4
3	4	2	1

1.

3			4
4			1

2.

4					1
		2	4		
	6	5	1	4	
	4	1	5	6	
		4	2		
1					4

TIME

....

SHAPE SKILLS

Let's put your shape skills to the test. All the following shapes, except one, have something in common. Work out what it is to find out which shape is the odd one out, then circle your answer.

What do the other shapes have in common? Write your answer here:

....

....

TIME

Spot all ten differences between these two pictures.

AGE DETECTIVE

Evie and Oscar are sister and brother. Use your super detective skills to work out how old they are from the following clues:

CLUES

1. When Oscar was three years old, Evie was less than twice as old as him.

2. There is more than one year age difference between them.

3. In two years' time, Oscar will be nine years old.

4. Oscar is younger than Evie.

Write your answer here:

Oscar is .... years old

Evie is .... years old

TIME

....

This word search is full of emotion! Find all 16 words listed below in the word search grid. Look horizontally, vertically, diagonally and backwards, too.

```
Y D T E I A E N V Y R O R
T A N N S E A N X I E T Y
I O R E A E R E A D E N V
S E Z E V A O I U R U E A
O S A O E F Y T U T C F S
I S L F Y D I S H N F U R
R E O O S T A G A E R E T
U N J I A E I Y C P R U A
C I A R L L O T R H A I N
R P G P E N I I H O R N G
I P E D N O S N I P U J E
A A L A N E A T F E I I R
I H E P R L R E D N O W E
```

AFFECTION
ANGER
ANNOYANCE
ANXIETY
CURIOSITY
DELIGHT
ENVY
FEAR

GRATITUDE
HAPPINESS
HOPE
JOY
LOVE
PLEASURE
SURPRISE
WONDER

TIME

SHAPE SPIN

Rotate pictures 1, 2 and 3 by 90° in a clockwise direction. Which option shows the rotated picture?

If you find this tricky, try turning the book clockwise so that the top right corner becomes the bottom right. Then turn the book back and choose the matching picture.

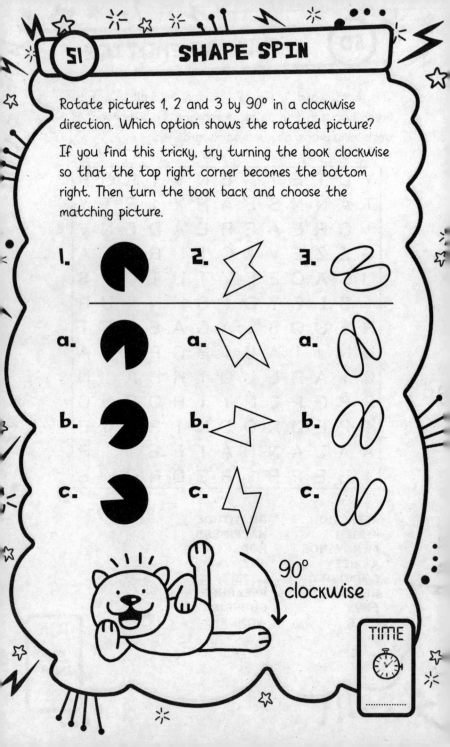

1.

2.

3.

a.

a.

a.

b.

b.

b.

c.

c.

c.

90° clockwise

TIME

LINKING LOOPS

Can you draw a single loop passing through every white square? Your moves must be horizontal or vertical and you can only visit each square once. You cannot cross over the loop.

EXAMPLE:

TIME

ANIMAL MAGIC

How good are you at spotting animals? Each of the words in this list has the name of an animal hiding in it. The letters are in the correct order so you don't have to jumble them up to find the creatures.

EXAMPLE: <u>bat</u>tery = bat

1. locate = ...

2. accelerate = ...

3. grapefruit = ...

4. freshener = ...

These words each have two animals hiding in them. Can you spot them all?

5. scowling = ... and ....

6. pigeonhole = ... and ....

TIME

....

NUMBER SEQUENCES

Test your super sequencing skills by filling in the missing numbers.

EXAMPLE:

3   11   19   27   35   _43_

Each number in the example sequence is equal to the previous number plus eight.

1. 1   5   9   13   17   ....

2. 48   43   38   33   28   ....

3. 17   23   29   35   41   ....

4. 66   55   44   33   22   ....

TIME

....

JEWEL HUNT

Can you find the jewels hidden in the empty squares of these puzzles? The numbers in the grid tell you how many jewels are hidden in the squares, horizontally, vertically and diagonally next to it. The example shows you how it works.

EXAMPLE:

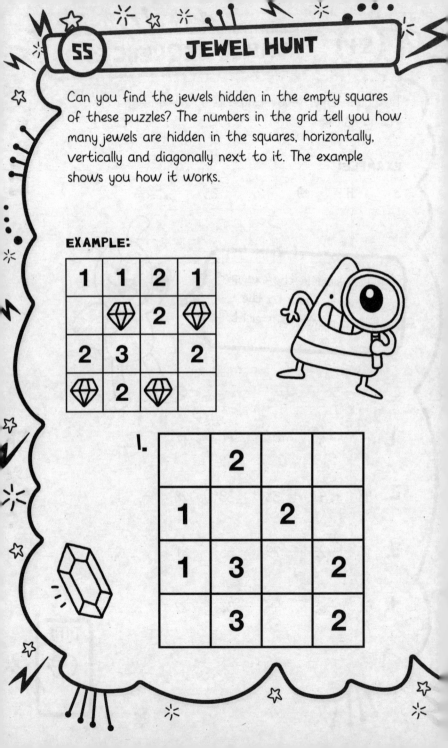

I.

2.

2			1
	4	2	1
	2	1	
1	1		

3.

2		3		1
4		5	2	
				1
	4	3		
1	2		2	

TIME

ROBOT MAZE

Can you help the robot find its way safely through this tricky maze?

Start

Finish

TIME

ODD WORD OUT

Can you circle the odd one out in each of the following sets? In the example, 'funny' is the odd one out because the other words in the set mean 'intelligent'.

EXAMPLE:

(funny)   wise   clever   smart

1. cabbage   apple   potato   parsnip

2. pen   ruler   pencil   crayon

3. drinking   dashing   doubtful   doubling

4. bee   oh   gold   pea

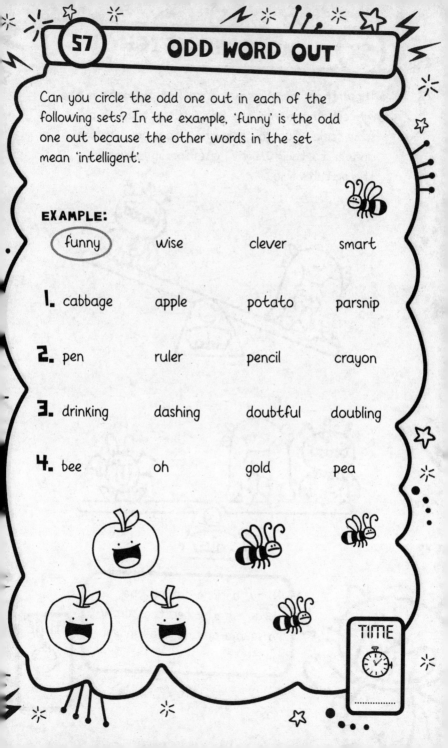

MONSTER WEIGH-IN

These three monsters want to find out who is the lightest and who is the heaviest, so they sit on some scales. Can you help them to work out the answer to their weighty question by looking at the pictures below?

Draw a circle around the heaviest monster, then draw a square around the lightest monster.

TIME

ANAGRAMS

How do you turn a DEN into an END? By mixing the letters up, of course! This is an example of an 'anagram'. Write an anagram for each of the words in capitals to complete the sentences.

EXAMPLE:

My play DEN is at one <u>END</u> of the living room.

1. Sometimes I meow and ACT as if I am a ....

2. The baby FOAL ate my .... of bread.

3. There was a big .... of PLUM inside my cake.

4. The LAMP shone light on the .... of my hand.

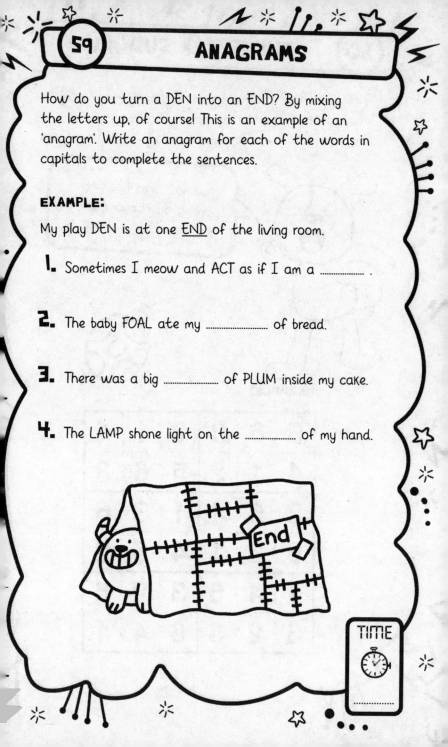

TIME

....

SUPER SIX SUDOKU

These 'super six' sudoku puzzles will really test your brain power! Place the numbers 1 to 6 into the grids so they appear once in every row, column and 3 x 2 area.

A 3 x 2 area has been circled on the example to help you.

EXAMPLE:

5	6	3	2	1	4
4	1	2	5	6	3
2	5	4	1	3	6
6	3	1	4	5	2
1	4	6	3	2	5
3	2	5	6	4	1

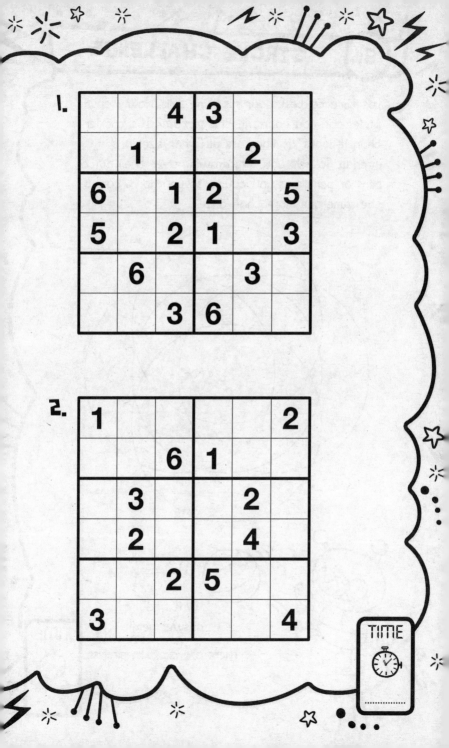

1.

		4	3		
	1			2	
6		1	2		5
5		2	1		3
	6			3	
		3	6		

2.

1					2
		6	1		
	3			2	
	2			4	
		2	5		
3					4

TIME

It's time to test your spotting skills. How many circles can you count in this picture? It's trickier than it looks, as they are different sizes and overlap. To help you, try drawing over them with pens or pencils as you count, so you don't count the same one more than once.

Write your answer here:

There are .... circles

TIME

....

TOUCHY NUMBERS

Each square in this puzzle should contain a number from 1 to 5. Can you fill in the missing numbers?

You cannot place the same number in touching, or diagonally-touching squares. Start with the middle square and work your way outwards to work out which numbers are needed.

	4		1	
2		5		4
	3		2	
4		1		3
	5		4	

SHAPE FOLDING

Two of these four shapes could be cut out and folded along the black lines to make a complete, six-sided cube. The other two could not.

Without cutting them out, can you work out which two could be folded to make cubes?

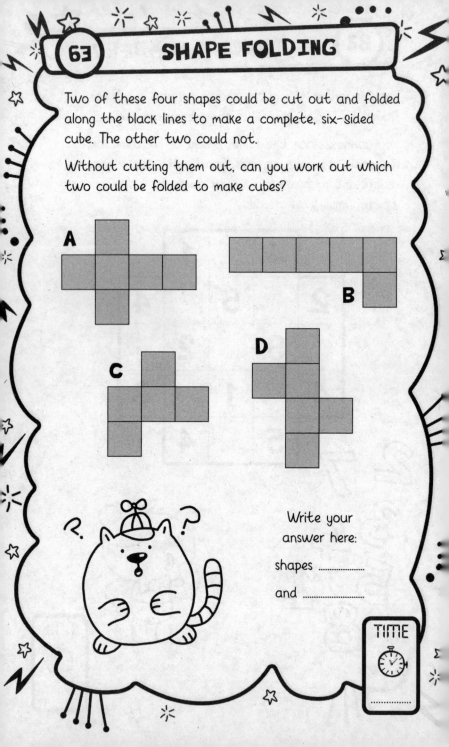

A

B

C

D

Write your answer here:

shapes ....

and ....

TIME

....

TIME TEASERS

It's time to take a look at the time! Let's see how you get on with these time-related problems.

1. You eat breakfast, then eat lunch four hours later and then eat dinner five hours after lunch. If you eat dinner at 6 p.m., what time did you eat breakfast? ....

2. You go to bed at 8 p.m. and wake up at 2 a.m., then go back to sleep for the same amount of time you've already been in bed. At what time will you next wake up? ....

3. You arrange to meet your friend at a time that is exactly halfway between 9 a.m. and 5 p.m. What time do you meet? ....

TIME
....

PICNIC PUZZLE

Draw two straight lines to divide this picnic blanket into four areas, so that each hungry monster has a sandwich and a cupcake.

TIME

....

WORD CIRCLE

There are several different words hidden in this word circle. Every word you find in the word circle must use the 'S' from the middle of the circle, plus three or more of the other letters.

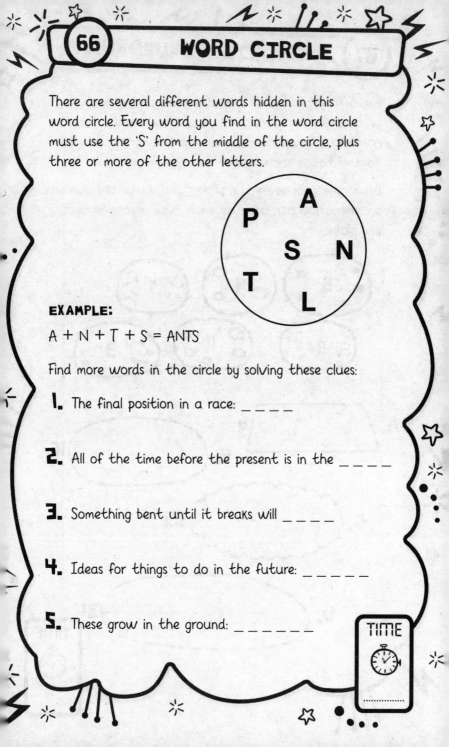

P A
S N
T
L

EXAMPLE:

A + N + T + S = ANTS

Find more words in the circle by solving these clues:

1. The final position in a race: _ _ _ _

2. All of the time before the present is in the _ _ _ _

3. Something bent until it breaks will _ _ _ _

4. Ideas for things to do in the future: _ _ _ _ _

5. These grow in the ground: _ _ _ _ _ _

TIME

Six different types of special number cookie need to be arranged on the plates below. You'll need to choose carefully so that the numbers on the cookies add up to the totals shown next to each plate.

Draw the cookies on the plates and write the numbers on them. You can only use each type of cookie once per plate.

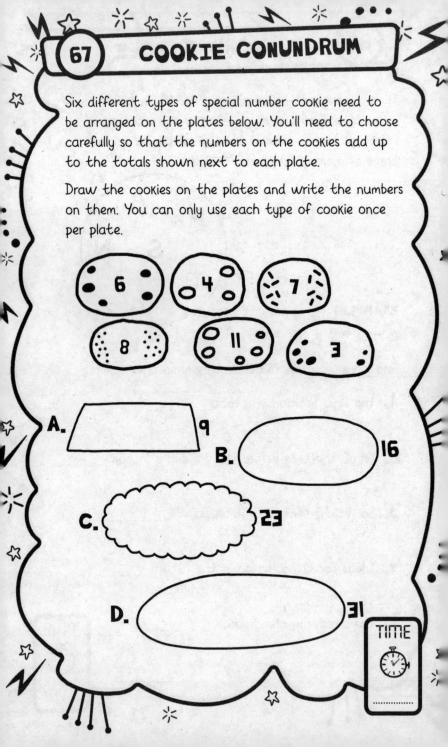

6

4

7

8

11

3

A. 9

B. 16

C. 23

D. 31

TIME
....

JIGSAW GRID

Fill in the empty spaces in the grid so that the letters A, B, C, D and E appear once in every row and column.

You must also ensure that the letters A to E appear once in each of the bold jigsaw-shaped areas.

To help you, one of the jigsaw shapes is circled in the example.

EXAMPLE:

A	B	E	D	C
B	E	D	C	A
C	A	B	E	D
E	D	C	A	B
D	C	A	B	E

	D			B
	E		C	
E		C		D
	C		D	
	A		E	

TIME

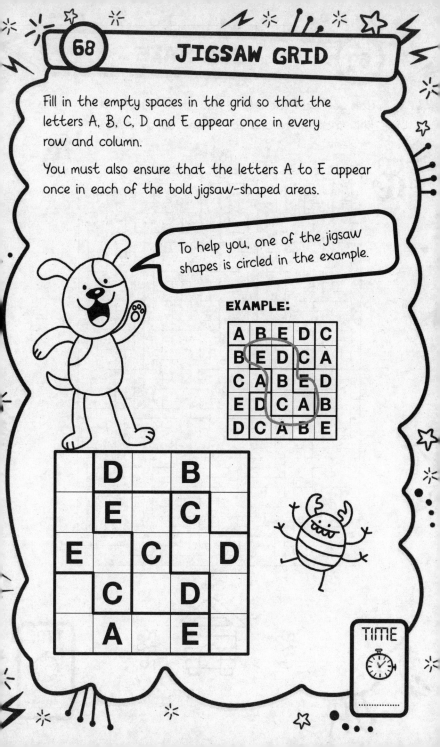

SPY SECRETS

This detective has received a coded message. Can you crack the code and find out where and when he should meet his contact?

To crack the code, replace each letter with the letter that comes two places after it in the alphabet. So, you would replace 'A' with 'C', and 'K' with 'M' for example. Write your answer in the space below.

KCCR

RMKMPPMU

GL RFC

RSLLCJ

WRITE YOUR ANSWER HERE:

_ _ _ _   _ _ _ _ _ _ _   _ _   _ _ _   _ _ _ _ _ _

A B C D E F G H I
J K L M N O P Q R
S T U V W X Y Z

TIME

LINKING SHAPES

Draw lines to join each pair of identical shapes. Lines must be horizontal or vertical, with just one line per square.

EXAMPLE:

1.

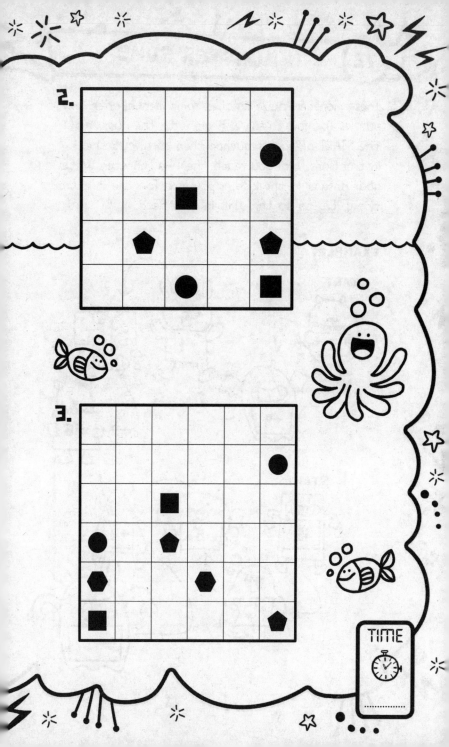

MONSTER SUMS

These monsters have created some mental arithmetic puzzles for you to solve. Begin with the number at the START of each sequence then carry out the instructions until you reach the final monster. Write your answer in the last empty box. To make it extra tricky, try to do the sums in your head.

EXAMPLE:

START

1. START

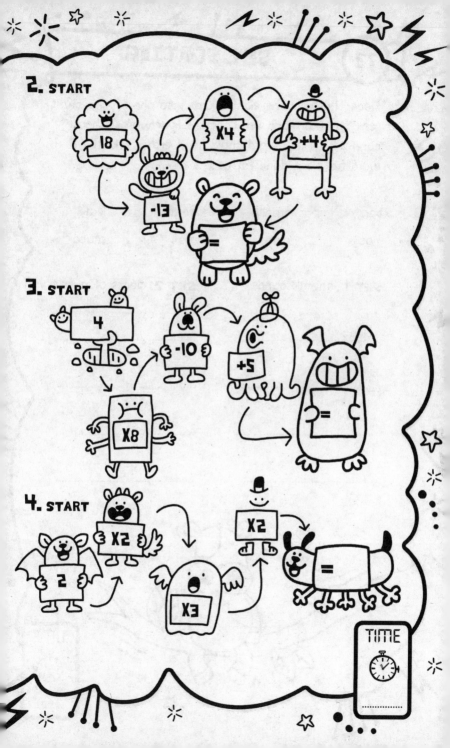

SET SORTING

Place the following eight words into one of the two sets, so that each set contains four words. Choose carefully, as one word could go in either set. The first word has been done for you.

bark   branch   bleat   leaf

moo   oink   root   squeak

SET 1: animal sounds   **SET 2:** parts of a tree

bleat
....

....

....

....

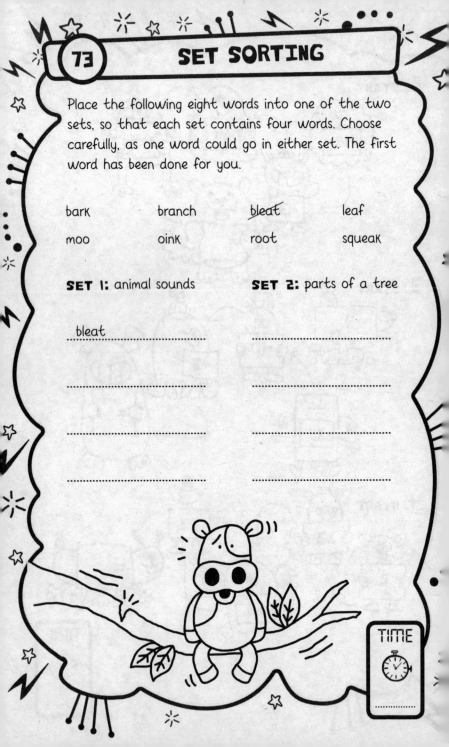

TIME
....

CALENDAR CONFUSION

Do you know your dates? Answer these calendar questions to find out:

1. It's 5th January today, and you arrange to meet your friend on 27th January. How many days from today are there until you meet your friend?

....

2. There are 30 days in September. Today is Tuesday 28th September. What day of the month will the first Monday in October be?

....

3. February has 29 days in a leap year. If it is a leap year, and the first day in February is a Wednesday, what day of the week will the last day of February be?

....

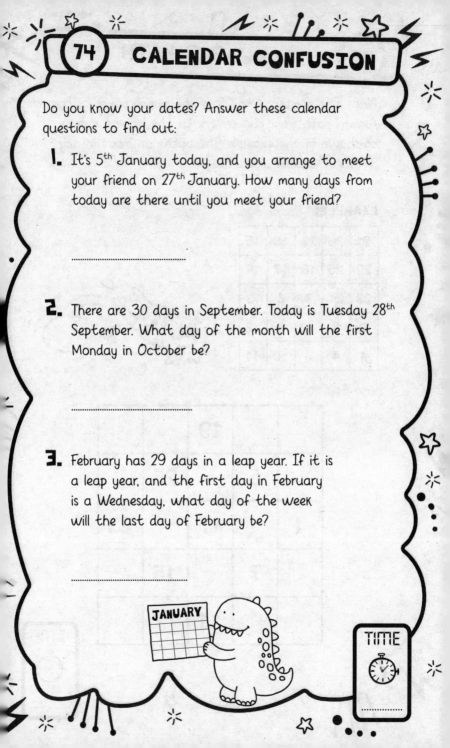

NUMBER PATH

Place the numbers 1 to 25 in the empty boxes so they form a path from the lowest to the highest number, as shown in the example. The path can move in any direction, except diagonally.

EXAMPLE:

21	20	19	16	15
22	25	18	17	14
23	24	7	8	13
2	3	6	9	12
1	4	5	10	11

		19		
	5		25	
1		17		23
	7		15	
		11		

TIME
....

SNEAKY WORDSEARCH

Test your spotting skills with this sneaky wordsearch. Find the 16 countries hidden in the grid. The words can be horizontal, vertical, diagonal or backwards.

```
S A I M P O L A N D I J P
C W C A E I K Z A M B I A
F A I H W K D G G C M L M
Y I A T I W Y R C N I R E
K N J N Z N E X Z Z Z G E
R E A I C E A C A M Y G S
A I N M C W R R B P F C T
M C O E R A B L T R T E O
N A C C J E E N A P A J N
E N M K I U G N P N N I I
D A M M R X C I Z E D J A
O D E E I E D R G N X K
P A P D R D M M M S I A A
```

BRAZIL   GERMANY
CANADA   GREECE
CHINA   JAPAN
DENMARK   MEXICO
EGYPT   PERU
ESTONIA   POLAND
FIJI   SWITZERLAND
FRANCE   ZAMBIA

TIME

Fill in the empty numbers to complete these pyramids. Each number must equal the sum of the numbers in the two blocks directly beneath.

So, in the example, 10 and 6 on the bottom line add up to 16 in the box above them.

EXAMPLE:

30	
16	14
10	6	8

I.

10	
	5	2

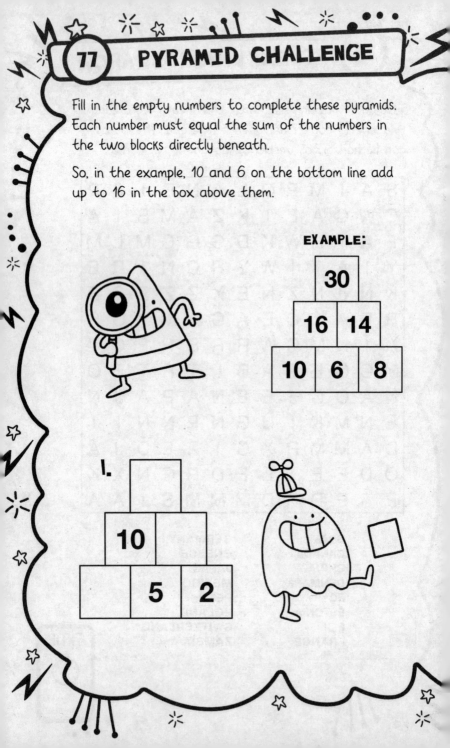

2.

	21	
	10	
		2

3.

	12	12	
			6
			3

4.

25			
	14		
		8	
			4

TIME

PICTURE MERGE

Imagine merging these two pictures, so that the white squares in picture A were replaced with the filled squares in picture B.

How many balloons would you be able to count in the merged picture?

A.

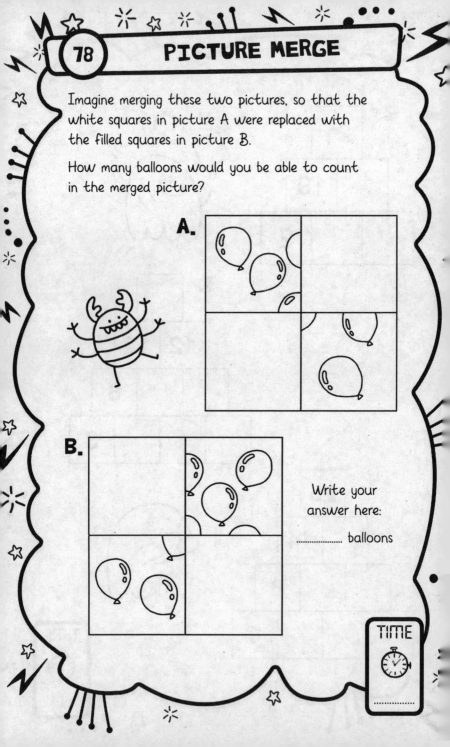

B.

Write your answer here:

.... balloons

TIME

....

PAINT MATCH

Each of the words in the left column is a shade of one of the paints in the right column.

Can you draw a line to match up each shade to the correct paint? The first one has been done for you.

crimson	black
ebony	blue
emerald	brown
navy	green
rose	pink
tan	purple
violet	red

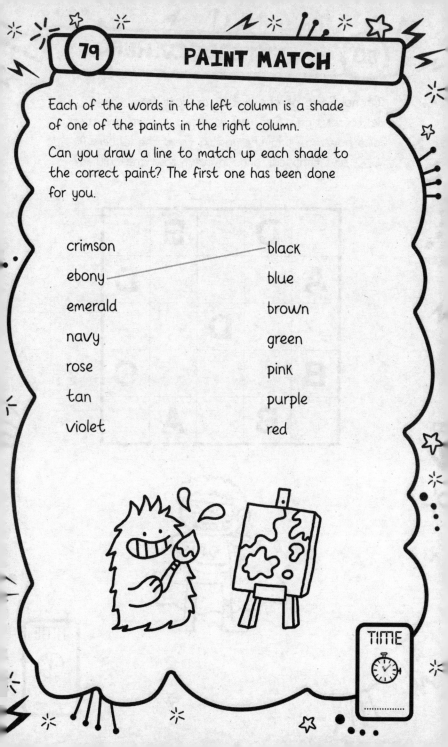

TIME

LETTERDOKU HERO

Oh no! Some of the letters are lost from this letterdoku grid. Can you be a puzzle hero and work out how to fill in the grid so that the letters A, B, C, D, and E appear once in every row and column?

	D		B	
A				D
		D		
B				C
	B		A	

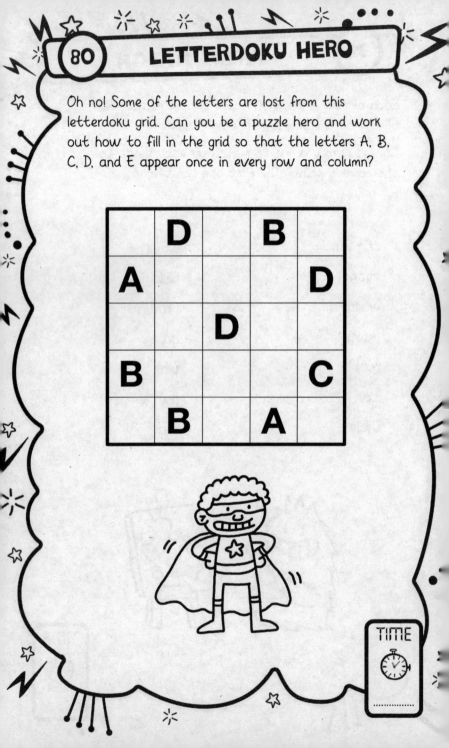

TIME

MARBLE MATHS

There are two different types of marble bag. Each different type of bag contains a different number of marbles, but the same type of bag always contains the same number of marbles.

If you buy the following bags, you would have 22 marbles:

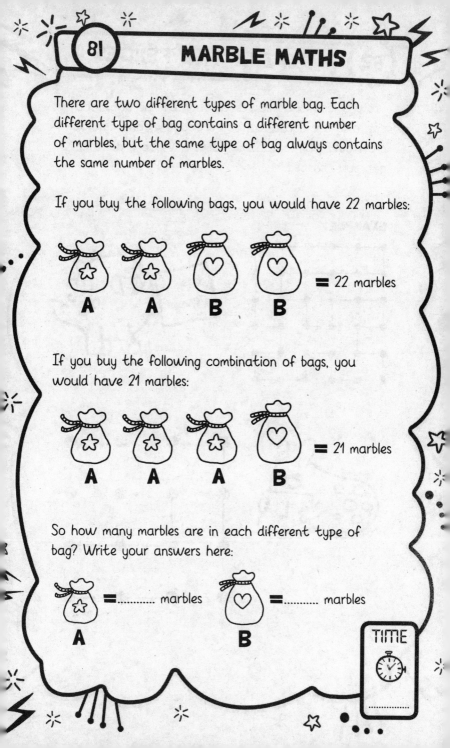

A   A   B   B   = 22 marbles

If you buy the following combination of bags, you would have 21 marbles:

A   A   A   B   = 21 marbles

So how many marbles are in each different type of bag? Write your answers here:

= .... marbles   = ... marbles

A   B

TIME

....

FINISH THE FENCES

Draw a loop that passes through all the dots. You can only use horizontal or vertical lines and cannot cross over the loop. Some parts have been done to get you started.

EXAMPLE:

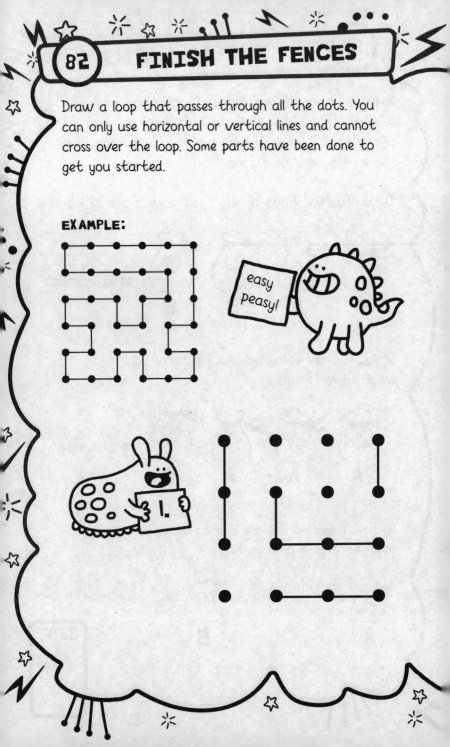

easy peasy!

I.

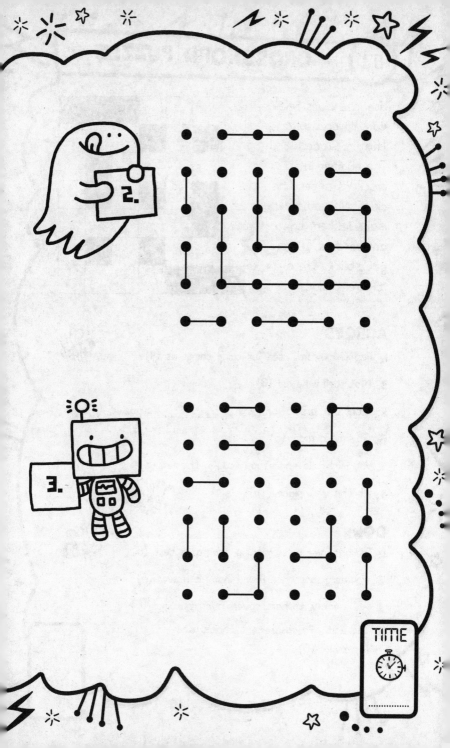

CROSSWORD PUZZLE

Use the clues below to help you solve this crossword. The number in brackets after the clue tells you how many letters the answer has. If you get stuck, try a different clue.

ACROSS

1. Very thick cord, used for tying things up (4)

3. Not well behaved (3)

5. Work out a solution, as in '_____ a puzzle' (5)

6. Go into a room (5)

7. You might do this if you stay in the sun (3)

8. At this very place (4)

DOWN

1. The outcome of something, such as a test (6)

2. Powdery substance found inside a flower (6)

3. An insect with hard covers over its wings (6)

4. The unit of measurement that's used for angles (6)

TIME

....

ALL THE ANSWERS

ANSWERS

BRAIN GAME 1

BRAIN GAME 2

O	P	T		M	U	S	I	C
W		A		A		A		A
E	R	R	O	R		N	U	N
		A		M		D		O
P	I	N	E	A	P	P	L	E
R		T		L		A		
E	M	U		A	P	P	L	E
S		L		D		E		A
S	C	A	R	E		R	A	T

BRAIN GAME 3

1. a. The friends have two pieces of chocolate each.

   b. Two pieces are left over.

2. The bar contained 14 pieces of chocolate.

BRAIN GAME 4

1. acti<u>on</u>ed = one
2. ar<u>two</u>rk = two
3. <u>ten</u>nis = ten
4. underw<u>eight</u> = eight
5. femi<u>nine</u> = nine
6. trus<u>two</u>rthy = two

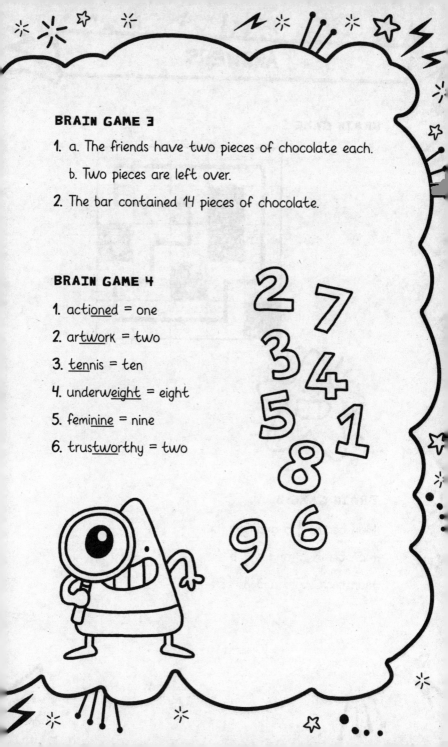

ANSWERS

BRAIN GAME 5

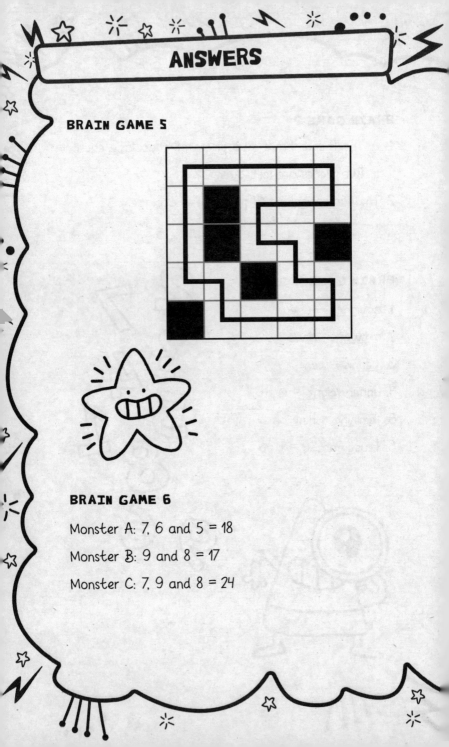

BRAIN GAME 6

Monster A: 7, 6 and 5 = 18

Monster B: 9 and 8 = 17

Monster C: 7, 9 and 8 = 24

BRAIN GAME 7

ANSWERS

BRAIN GAME 8

BRAIN GAME 9

1.

2.

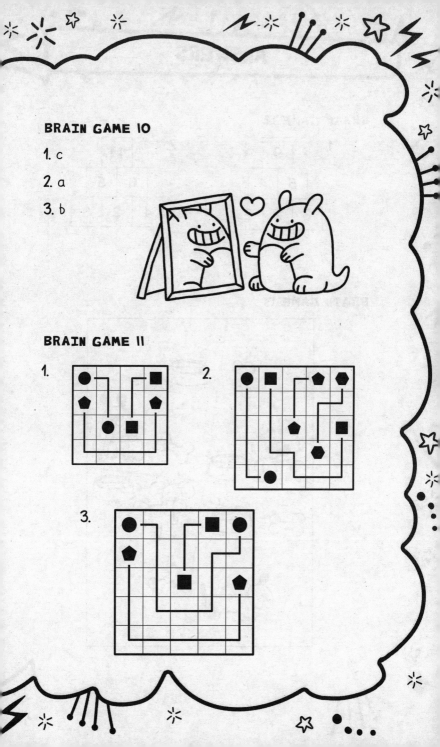

ANSWERS

BRAIN GAME 12

1.

```
      9
   5     4
 3    2    2
```

2.

```
      11
    6     5
  4    2    3
```

BRAIN GAME 13

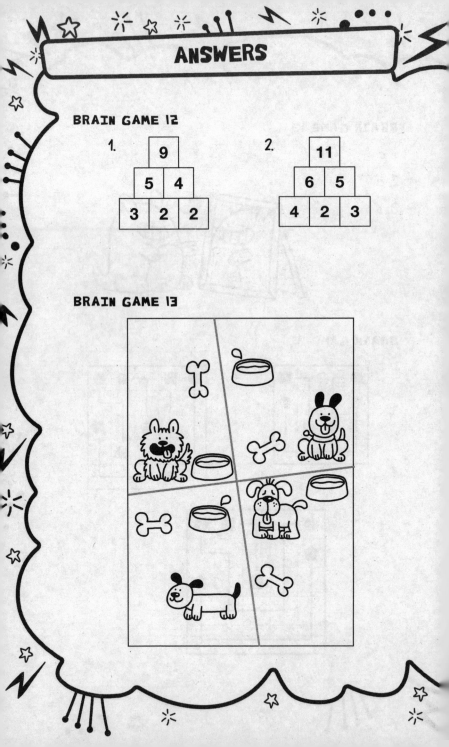

BRAIN GAME 14

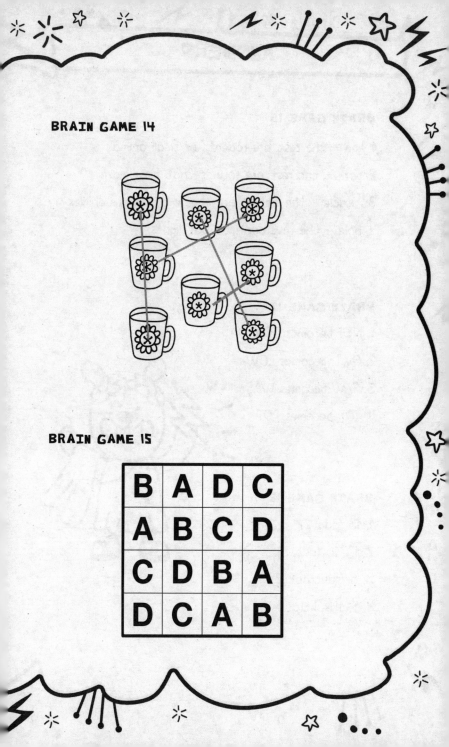

BRAIN GAME 15

B	A	D	C
A	B	C	D
C	D	B	A
D	C	A	B

ANSWERS

BRAIN GAME 16

1. lion – the rest are rodents or small animals

2. bark – the rest are sounds that birds make

3. bicycle – the others are engine-powered vehicles

4. hole – the rest can give out light

BRAIN GAME 17

1. NET becomes TEN

2. OWL becomes LOW

3. SAW becomes WAS

4. TOP becomes POT

BRAIN GAME 18

1. 13 (add 2)

2. 13, 16 (add 3)

3. 6 (subtract 2)

4. 5, 1 (subtract 4)

BRAIN GAME 19

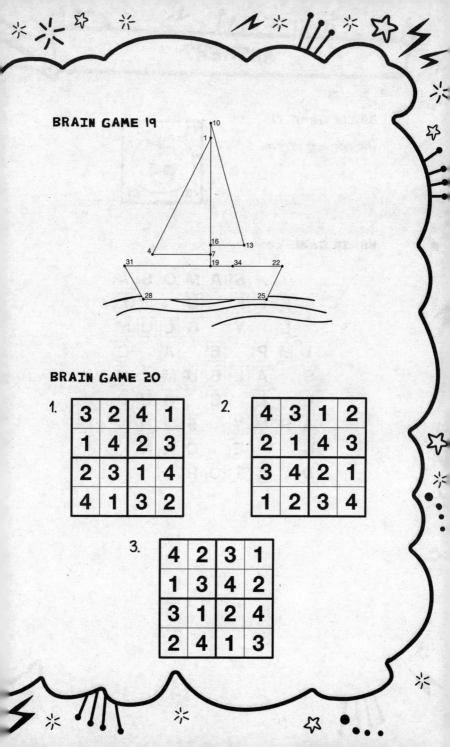

BRAIN GAME 20

1.

3	2	4	1
1	4	2	3
2	3	1	4
4	1	3	2

2.

4	3	1	2
2	1	4	3
3	4	2	1
1	2	3	4

3.

4	2	3	1
1	3	4	2
3	1	2	4
2	4	1	3

BRAIN GAME 21

The correct picture is 1:

BRAIN GAME 22

```
      S A M O S A
  E L K   U     L
  L   Y   G L U M
 I M P   E   A   O
 S   A L B U M   N
 S   L   B   B U D
 A R M Y   F   R
 N   E   O W N
 D O C T O R
```

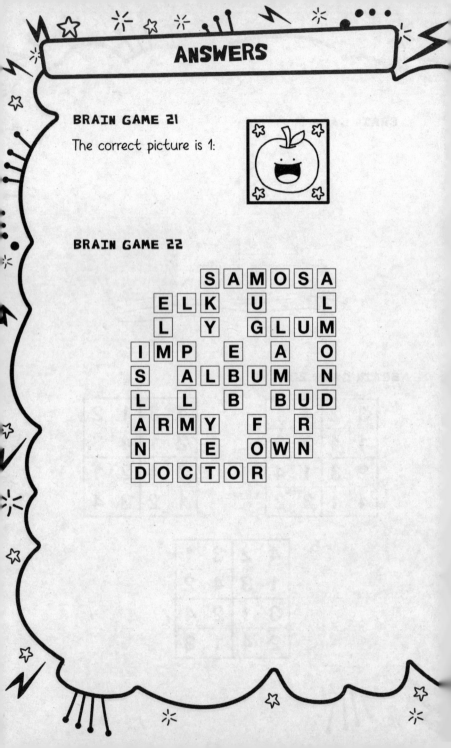

BRAIN GAME 23

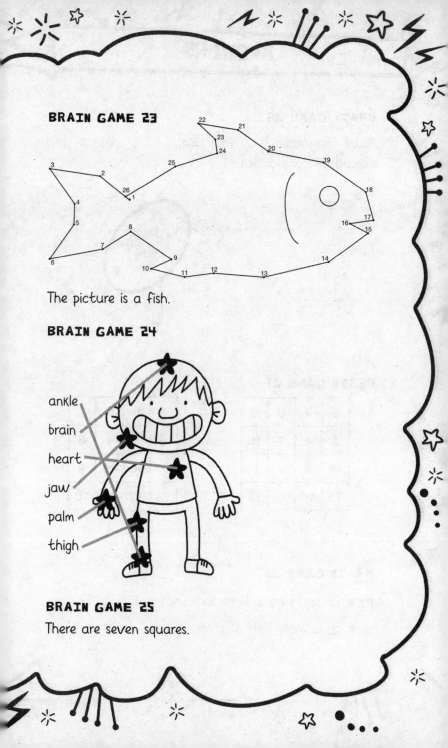

The picture is a fish.

BRAIN GAME 24

ankle
brain
heart
jaw
palm
thigh

BRAIN GAME 25

There are seven squares.

ANSWERS

BRAIN GAME 26

All of the shapes have four sides,
except the one circled:

BRAIN GAME 27

1.

6	7	8	9
5	4	1	10
16	3	2	11
15	14	13	12

2.

4	5	6	7
3	2	1	8
14	15	16	9
13	12	11	10

BRAIN GAME 28

SET 1. sports equipment: boot, ball, net, racket

SET 2. animals: bat, dog, lion, mouse

BRAIN GAME 29

1. 5 cats are standing on four legs

2. 4 cats with striped tails are sleeping

3. 3 cats are washing

4. 2 cats are chasing mice

BRAIN GAME 30

contains two pieces of chocolate

contains three pieces of chocolate

BRAIN GAME 31

B	A	D	E	C
C	E	A	D	B
E	D	C	B	A
A	B	E	C	D
D	C	B	A	E

BRAIN GAME 32

1. ANT

2. RAT

3. AIR

4. RAIN

5. TRAIN

ANSWERS

BRAIN GAME 33

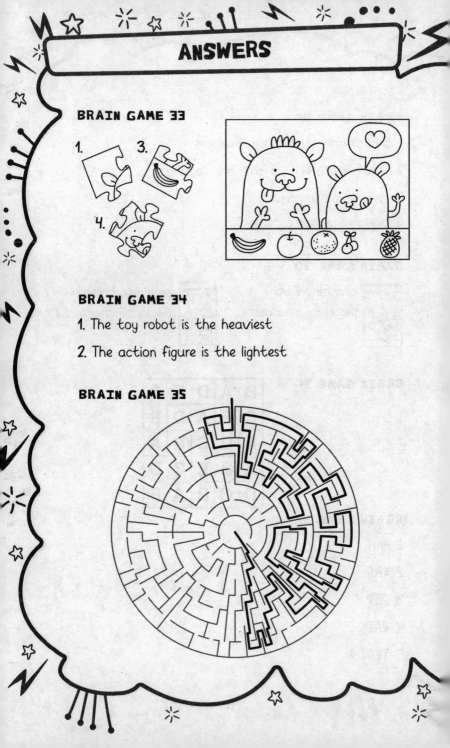

BRAIN GAME 34

1. The toy robot is the heaviest

2. The action figure is the lightest

BRAIN GAME 35

BRAIN GAME 36

1.

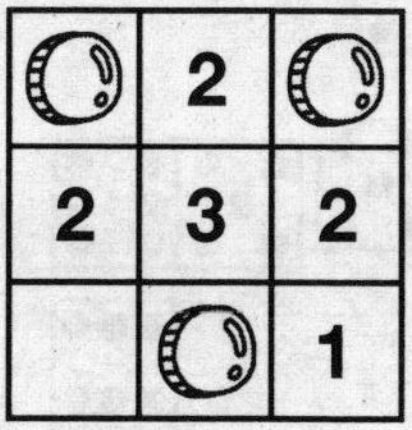

🔵	2	🔵
2	3	2
	🔵	1

2.

🔵	2	2	2
1		🔵	🔵
2		4	3
🔵	🔵	🔵	1

BRAIN GAME 37

1. a

2. a

3. b

BRAIN GAME 38

The message reads:

Under the tall oak tree

BRAIN GAME 39

Vase A: 3 and 9 = 12

Vase B: 6 and 10 = 16

Vase C: 5, 6 and 9 = 20

Vase D: 5, 6, 9 and 10 = 30

ANSWERS

BRAIN GAME 40

The odd one out is:

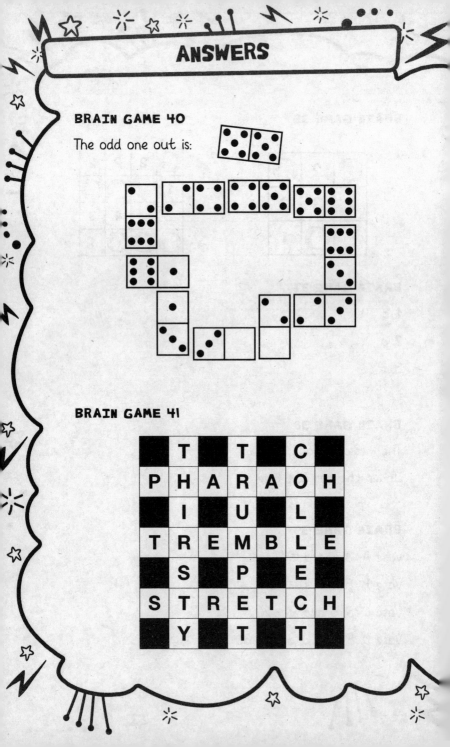

BRAIN GAME 41

BRAIN GAME 42

The picture is a smiley face.

1	**2**	3	**4**	5
6	7	8	9	10
11	12	**13**	14	15
16	17	18	19	**20**
21	**22**	**23**	**24**	25

BRAIN GAME 43

1. 10 〉 15 〉 = 7
2. 30 〉 20 〉 = 25
3. 6 〉 24 〉 = 27
4. 24 〉 36 〉 = 32

ANSWERS

BRAIN GAME 44

1. 10e + 5e

2. 2e, 2e and 1e

3. 5 coins: 20e + 20e + 10e + 2e + 2e

4. a. five 1e coins

   b. one 2e coin and three 1e coins

   c. one 5e coin

BRAIN GAME 45

1. b

2. c

3. c

BRAIN GAME 46

1.

3	1	2	4
2	4	1	3
1	3	4	2
4	2	3	1

2.

4	5	3	6	2	1
6	1	2	4	3	5
3	6	5	1	4	2
2	4	1	5	6	3
5	3	4	2	1	6
1	2	6	3	5	4

BRAIN GAME 47

The sides of each shape are the same length, except for the shape that's ringed below.

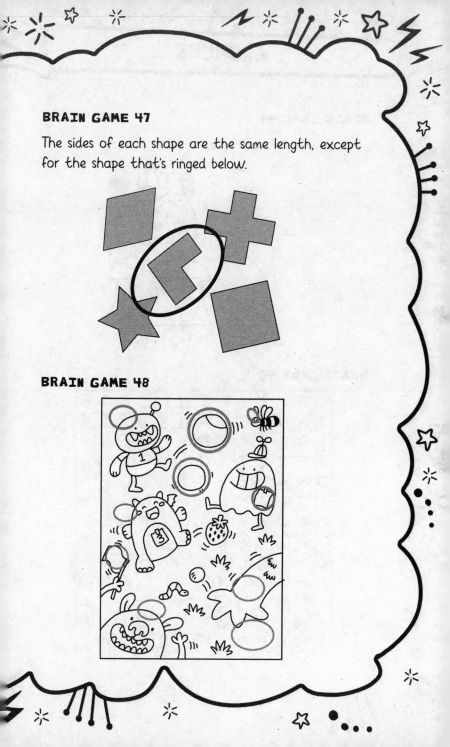

BRAIN GAME 48

ANSWERS

BRAIN GAME 49

Oscar is seven, Evie is nine.

BRAIN GAME 50

BRAIN GAME 51

1. b

2. a

3. a

BRAIN GAME 52

BRAIN GAME 53

1. lo<u>cate</u> = cat

2. accele<u>rate</u> = rat

3. gr<u>ape</u>fruit = ape

4. fresh<u>en</u>er = hen

5. sc<u>ow</u>ling and sc<u>owl</u>ing = cow and owl

6. <u>pig</u>eonhole and <u>pigeon</u>hole = pig and pigeon

ANSWERS

BRAIN GAME 54

1. 21 (add 4)
2. 23 (subtract 5)
3. 47 (add 6)
4. 11 (subtract 11)

BRAIN GAME 55

1.

💎	2	💎	
1		2	
	3	💎	2
💎	3	💎	2

2.

2	💎	💎	1
💎	4	2	1
💎	2	1	
1	1		💎

3.

2	💎	3	💎	1
4	💎	5	2	
💎	💎		💎	1
💎	4	3		
1	2	💎	2	💎

BRAIN GAME 56

BRAIN GAME 57

1. apple – the rest are vegetables

2. ruler – you can write or draw with the others

3. doubtful – the other words end in 'ing'

4. gold – the others sound like letters when read out: B, O and P

ANSWERS

BRAIN GAME 58

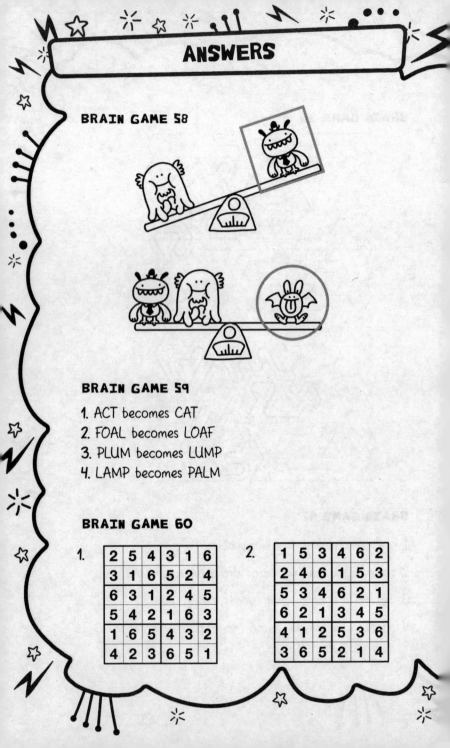

BRAIN GAME 59

1. ACT becomes CAT
2. FOAL becomes LOAF
3. PLUM becomes LUMP
4. LAMP becomes PALM

BRAIN GAME 60

1.

2	5	4	3	1	6
3	1	6	5	2	4
6	3	1	2	4	5
5	4	2	1	6	3
1	6	5	4	3	2
4	2	3	6	5	1

2.

1	5	3	4	6	2
2	4	6	1	5	3
5	3	4	6	2	1
6	2	1	3	4	5
4	1	2	5	3	6
3	6	5	2	1	4

BRAIN GAME 61

There are five circles.

BRAIN GAME 62

	4	2	1	
2	1	5	3	4
5	3	4	2	1
4	2	1	5	3
	5	3	4	

BRAIN GAME 63

Shapes A and D could be folded to make cubes.

BRAIN GAME 64

1. You ate lunch at 1 p.m., so you ate breakfast at 9 a.m.

2. You have been in bed for six hours already, so you will wake up at 8 a.m.

3. You arrange to meet your friend at 1 p.m.

ANSWERS

BRAIN GAME 65

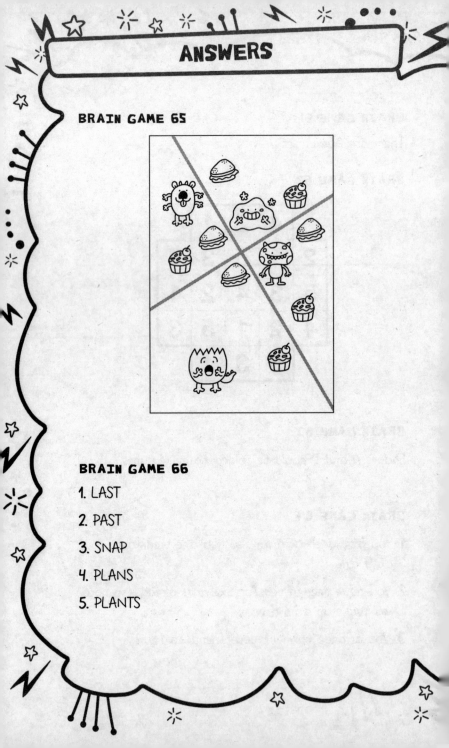

BRAIN GAME 66

1. LAST
2. PAST
3. SNAP
4. PLANS
5. PLANTS

BRAIN GAME 67

Plate A: 3 and 6 = 9

Plate B: 3, 6 and 7 = 16

Plate C: 4, 8 and 11 = 23

Plate D: 3, 4, 6, 7 and 11 = 31

BRAIN GAME 68

A	D	E	B	C
D	E	B	C	A
E	B	C	A	D
B	C	A	D	E
C	A	D	E	B

ANSWERS

BRAIN GAME 69

BRAIN GAME 70

The message says 'meet tomorrow in the tunnel'.

BRAIN GAME 71

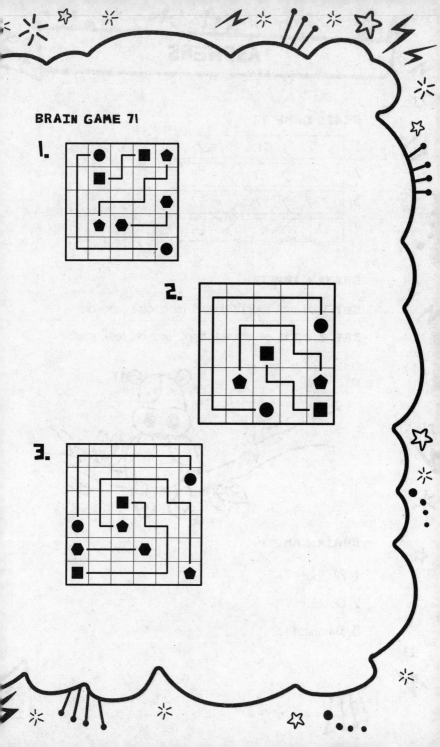

ANSWERS

BRAIN GAME 72

1. 27 > 21 > = 25
2. 5 > 20 > = 24
3. 32 > 22 > = 27
4. 4 > 12 > = 24

BRAIN GAME 73

SET 1. animal sounds: bleat, moo, oink, squeak

SET 2. parts of a tree: bark, branch, leaf, root

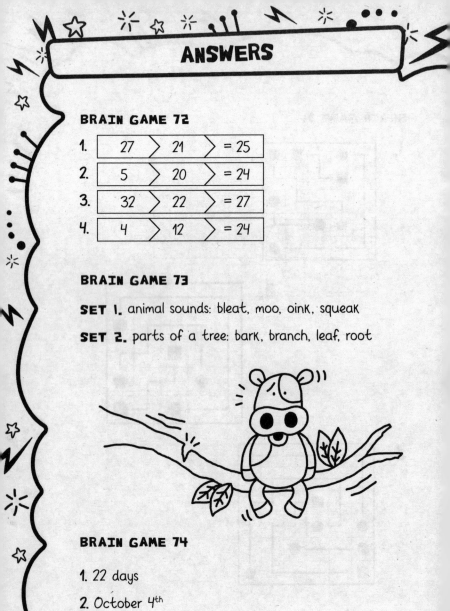

BRAIN GAME 74

1. 22 days
2. October 4th
3. Wednesday

BRAIN GAME 75

3	4	19	20	21
2	5	18	25	22
1	6	17	24	23
8	7	16	15	14
9	10	11	12	13

BRAIN GAME 76

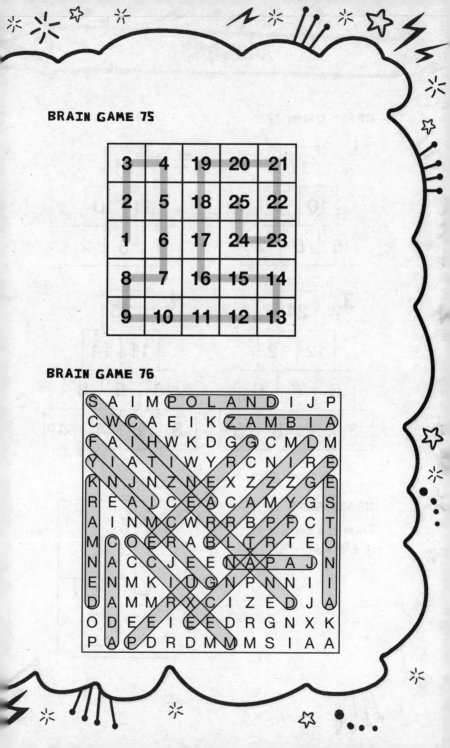

ANSWERS

BRAIN GAME 77

1.

```
      17
   10     7
  5    5    2
```

2.

```
      21
   11    10
  3    8    2
```

3.

```
       24
    12    12
   6    6    6
  3   3   3   3
```

4.

```
       25
    11    14
   5    6    8
  3   2   4   4
```

BRAIN GAME 78

There are ten balloons in the merged picture.

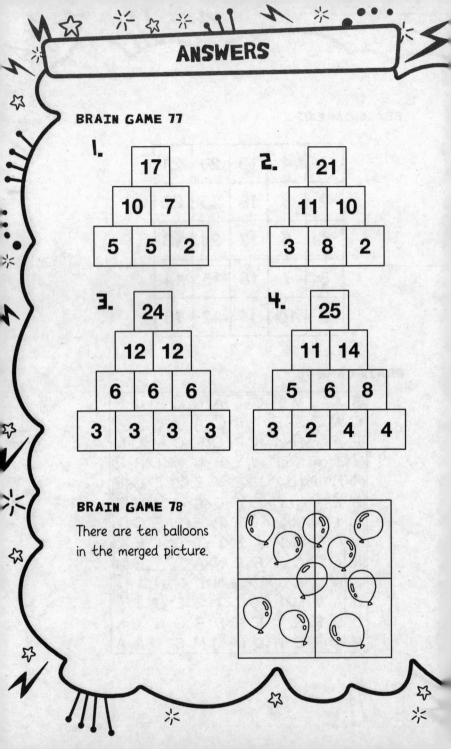

BRAIN GAME 79

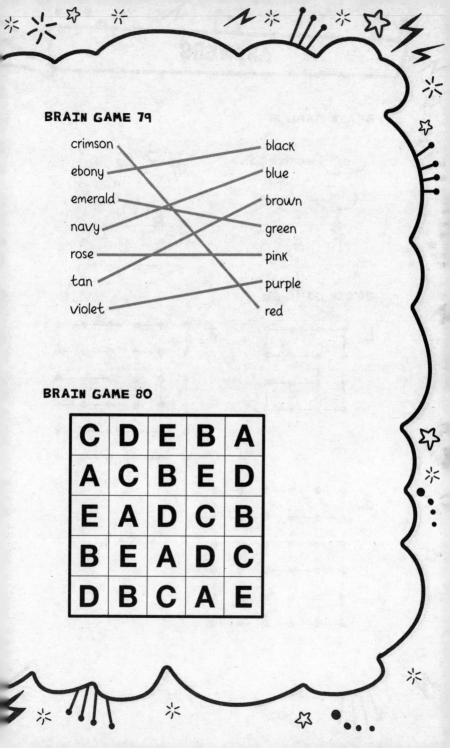

crimson — green
ebony — brown
emerald — blue
navy — black
rose — pink
tan — red
violet — purple

BRAIN GAME 80

C	D	E	B	A
A	C	B	E	D
E	A	D	C	B
B	E	A	D	C
D	B	C	A	E

ANSWERS

BRAIN GAME 81

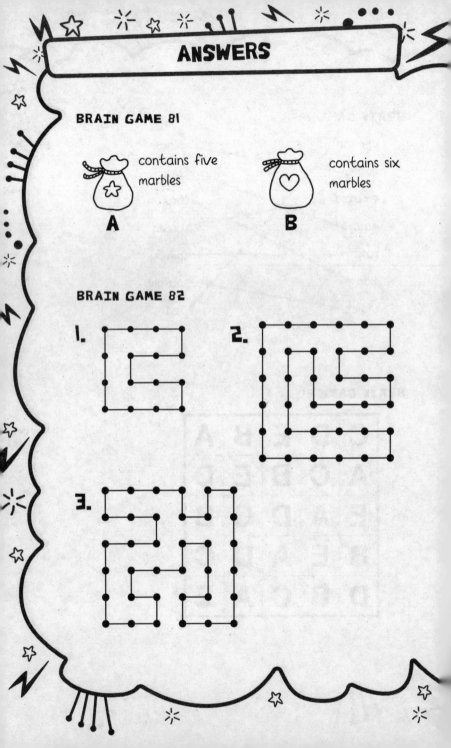 contains five marbles

A

contains six marbles

B

BRAIN GAME 82

1.

2.

3.

BRAIN GAME 83

R	O	P	E			
E		O		B	A	D
S	O	L	V	E		E
U		L		E		G
L		E	N	T	E	R
T	A	N		L		E
			H	E	R	E

NOTES AND SCRIBBLES

NOTES

NOTES

NOTES

NOTES

NOTES

NOTES

NOTES

NOTES

NOTES

NOTES